Rereading the Biblical Text

Rereading the Biblical Text

Searching for Meaning and Understanding

Claude F. Mariottini

WIPF & STOCK · Eugene, Oregon

REREADING THE BIBLICAL TEXT
Searching for Meaning and Understanding

Wipf & Stock
An Imprint of Wipf and Stock Publishers
199 W. 8th Ave., Suite 3
Eugene, OR 97401

www.wipfandstock.com

ISBN 13: 978-1-62032-827-9

Manufactured in the U.S.A.

This book is dedicated to my wife Donna.

Contents

Acknowledgments

I WANT TO EXPRESS my gratitude to Northern Baptist Seminary and the Board of Trustees for granting me a sabbatical leave, which provided study time to research and complete this project. I also want to thank my former student John Withum for reading and editing an earlier version of this manuscript and my friend Michael J. Clemens for preparing the indexes. My wife Donna has done most of the work in reading, editing, and typing the manuscript. I am grateful for her faithful work and her support in helping me bring this project to completion.

Lombard, December 2012
Claude F. Mariottini

Abbreviations

ASV American Standard Version (1901)
BBE English Bible in Basic English
BDB Brown, F., S. R. Driver, and C. A. Briggs, *A Hebrew and English Lexicon of the Old Testament.*
BHK *Biblia Hebraica.* Edited by R. Kittel.
BHS *Biblia Hebraica Stuttgartensia.* Edited by K. Elliger and W. Rudolph.
CEB Common English Bible
CJB Complete Jewish Bible
DBY English Darby Bible
DRA Douay-Rheims (1899) American Edition
ERV English Revised Version
ESV English Standard Version
GBV Geneva Bible (1599)
GKC *Gesenius's Hebrew Grammar.* Edited by E. Kautzsch. Translated by A. E. Cowley.
GNB Good News Bible
GWN God's Word to the Nations
HCSB Holman Christian Standard Bible
JPS Holy Scriptures, Jewish Publication Society (1917)
KB Koehler, L. and W. Baumgartner, *The Hebrew and Aramaic Lexicon of the Old Testament.*
KJV King James Version
LXX Septuagint
MT Masoretic Text
NAB New American Bible
NASB New American Standard Bible
NEB New English Bible

NET	New English Translation
NirV	New International Reader's Version
NIV	New International Version
NJB	New Jerusalem Bible
NKJV	New King James Version
NLT	New Living Translation
NRSV	New Revised Standard Version Bible
REB	Revised English Bible
RSV	Revised Standard Version of the Bible
RWB	Revised Webster Update
TDOT	Botterweck, G. Johannes and Helmer Ringgren, eds. *Theological Dictionary of the Old Testament.*
TNIV	Today's New International Version
TNK	JPS Tanakh (1985)
YLT	Young's Literal Translation

Apocryphal/Deuterocanonical Book

Bar	Baruch
1 Mac	1 Maccabees
Wis	Wisdom of Solomon

Other Ancient Sources

B. Bat.	*Baba Batra*
Šabb.	*Šabbat*
Tg. Ps.-J.	*Targum Pseudo-Jonathan*

Scripture Abbreviations

Hebrew Bible / Old Testament:

Gen	Genesis	Song	Song of Solomon
Exod	Exodus	Isa	Isaiah
Lev	Leviticus	Jer	Jeremiah
Num	Numbers	Lam	Lamentations
Deut	Deuteronomy	Ezek	Ezekiel
Josh	Joshua	Dan	Daniel
Judg	Judges	Hos	Hosea
Ruth	Ruth	Joel	Joel
1–2 Sam	1–2 Samuel	Amos	Amos
1– 2 Kgs	1–2 Kings	Obad	Obadiah
1–2 Chr	1–2 Chronicles	Jonah	Jonah
Ezra	Ezra	Mic	Micah
Neh	Nehemiah	Nah	Nahum
Esth	Esther	Hab	Habakkuk
Job	Job	Zeph	Zephaniah
Ps	Psalm	Hag	Haggai
Prov	Proverbs	Zech	Zechariah
Eccl	Ecclesiastes	Mal	Malachi

New Testament:

Matt	Matthew	1–2 Thess	1–2 Thessalonians
Mark	Mark	1–2 Tim	1–2 Timothy
Luke	Luke	Titus	Titus
John	John	Philm	Philemon
Acts	Acts	Heb	Hebrews
Rom	Romans	Jas	James
1–2 Cor	1–2 Corinthians	1–2 Pet	1–2 Peter
Gal	Galatians	1–2–3 John	1–2–3 John
Eph	Ephesians	Jude	Jude
Phil	Philippians	Rev	Revelation
Col	Colossians		

Introduction

FOR MORE THAN TWO thousand years the Bible has played an important role in the life of the church. Because the faith community regards the Bible as the word of God, believers read and interpret the Bible as authoritative Scripture.

People who read the Bible learn important principles that will help them confront the many problems of life with confidence. However, people who want to do an in-depth study of the Bible will need to know some of the historical, political, religious, and social events that shaped the history of ancient Israel and molded later Israelite society.

It took many years for the Bible to come to its final shape. The Bible was written by many writers over a period of more than a thousand years. The name itself, *Biblia*, comes from a Greek word that means "books." The Bible is a collection of books bound in one volume.

Before the invention of the printing press, the books of the Bible were copied by hand by scribes who worked diligently to preserve the original reading of the manuscripts. However, when a document is copied by hand, it is inevitable that some errors of transmission will occur. A detailed study of extant manuscripts reveals that errors in copying were made by the scribes.

The aim of biblical scholars today is to compare the thousands of manuscripts that have survived and discover which text is the most accurate and which is closer to the original work produced by the biblical writer.

As scholars seek to reconstruct the biblical text, it becomes important to know that none of the original manuscripts of the Bible have survived. Thus, scholars work with the available manuscripts and try to reconstruct the text from the many variants in order to discover where the scribes made some unintentional errors. Although no text is perfect, students of the Bible can be confident that the text of the Bible available to us today is reliable and comes close to the original text.

The Hebrew text that became the basis for the Christian Old Testament is known as the Masoretic Text (MT). The Masoretes were a group of Jewish scholars who copied and preserved the manuscripts of the biblical books. Because the Masoretes believed the texts of those scrolls were sacred Scripture, they worked diligently to preserve the traditional reading and pronunciation of the text.

The word Masorah means tradition. The Masoretes made an attempt at preserving the original text. In order to accomplish their goal, they made several notations, and counted words and letters in the manuscripts in order to assure they were preserving and copying the correct text. When the Masoretes found a discrepancy in a manuscript, they wrote notes in the margins of the manuscript informing the reader of the problem they found. If the error was written in the text, they left the error in the text, but placed a note in the margin of the manuscript giving the correct reading of the text. In many places in these studies, readers will be reading about the *ketiv* and the *qere*.

The *ketiv* is what is written in the text. The *ketiv* reflects an error in the text that a scribe unintentionally introduced into the manuscript. In order to preserve the correct reading of the text, the scribe wrote a note in the margins of the manuscript and gave the correct reading of the text. This is the *qere*, or what should be read. In translating the Hebrew text into English, some translations follow the *ketiv* while others follow the *qere*. When this happens, the translations will differ in presenting the message of the biblical writer to the reader.

An important version of the Hebrew text is the Septuagint (LXX). The Septuagint was the Greek translation of the books of the Old Testament done in Egypt by seventy-two Jewish scholars who lived in Egypt. The Greek translation of the Hebrew texts began in the middle of the third-century B.C. and it was the Bible most Christians used when preaching the gospel to Gentiles who lived in the Roman Empire. Most English translations follow the Masoretic Text. However, some translations, following the example of the New Testament writers, depart from the Hebrew text and adopt some of the readings of the Septuagint. In these studies, I will mention a few places where English translations follow the translation of the Septuagint.

Readers who may not know Hebrew or Greek may think these problems of translation diminish the authority of the Bible. Although there are many variant readings in the Hebrew and Greek manuscripts and although scholars may disagree on how to translate a text, the authority of the Bible still remains and none of these difficulties pose a threat to Christian faith or doctrine.

The Bible was written in three languages. The Old Testament was written primarily in Hebrew with a few chapters written in Aramaic.[1] The New Testament was written in Greek.

Since most Christians do not know the biblical languages, they depend on translations of the Bible in order to read about the history of early Israel, the message of Christ, and the work of the apostles. The most popular translation of the Bible in the English language is the King James Version (KJV), also known as the Authorized Version. The KJV was published in 1611, but it was not the first English translation of the Bible.

The first English translation of the Bible was the Tyndale Bible (1526). The Coverdale Bible, published in 1535, was the first complete translation of the Bible into English. The Geneva Bible (GNV) was published in 1560 as it was the favorite Bible of the Puritans. The Douay Bible (DBA) is a very literal translation of the Latin Vulgate. It was first published in French. The quotes from the DBA in this book are taken from the 1899 American edition.

The King James Version (KJV) was published for use in the Church of England. The Bible takes its name from King James I of England who requested it. The KJV took into consideration previous translations and some of its translation was highly influenced by the Tyndale Bible. The discovery of new manuscripts and the need to modernize the language prompted a revision of the KJV in 1881. The American Standard Bible (ASV) was a revision of the KJV for an American audience and it was published in 1901. The Revised Standard Version (RSV) is a revision of the ASV, which was a revision of the KJV.

Translating the text of the Hebrew Bible for modern readers is a difficult task. The vocabulary and grammar of the Hebrew language are different from the grammar structure of the English language. In their book, *Introduction to Biblical Interpretation*, Klein, Blomberg, and Hubbard write: "All languages present their words in a system of grammatical and literary structures—sentences, paragraphs, poems, discourses, and even large units."[2] It is for this reason that knowledge of the original language becomes important if the reader wants to know what the biblical writer was trying to communicate to his audience. Because the biblical writers used idiomatic

---

1. The following passages in the Old Testament were written in Aramaic: Gen 31:47; Jer 10:11; Ezra 4:8–6:18; 7:12–26; Dan 2:4–7:28.

2. Klein, Blomberg, and Hubbard, *Introduction to Biblical Interpretation*, 9.

language that cannot be transferred into English, translators may translate a Hebrew word quite differently from what the biblical writers intended for their primary audience.

The primary goal of the translator of the text is to convey to a modern reader what the original author tried to convey to his original audience. As Klein, Blomberg, and Hubbard write: "If we are seeking the meaning intended by the author to the original recipients, that meaning must be the meaning they could understand at that time, not the meaning we would determine based on our position of advanced historical development."[3]

Many obscure and difficult readings are found in the Hebrew text. This happens because the text is either corrupt, the Hebrew word is unknown, or the intent of the original writers is not clear. When translators encounter these problems they may use one of the ancient languages to shed light on the possible intent of the author. In her book *Studying the Old Testament*, Annemarie Ohler writes: "We are compelled to observe that the translator at times has no English word at his disposal which has a similar range of significance as the Hebrew. Then no alternative is left except to try to grasp the meaning of the Hebrew word, and to infer from the context what part of the range of the word's meaning fits the passage of the text lying before us."[4]

In translating the Bible, the translator cannot introduce into the text a meaning influenced by Christian theology. "If we read into the biblical texts information the authors could not possess, we distort their meaning."[5] It is true that at times, the intent of the author's message is not self-evident. The original recipients of the biblical texts lived in a different historical and cultural setting. Translators must be careful not to inject contemporary ideas that may change what the original writer was trying to communicate to his audience.

Christians believe the Holy Spirit helps them read and understand the Bible. By faith believers can read and appropriate the message of the Bible and apply what they learned to their lives. The proper understanding of the message of the Bible begins with a personal relationship with God. Although reading the Bible from a faith-perspective provides a basic knowledge of the content of the Bible, this kind of reading may not provide a full understanding of the intent of the author. There are many reasons for this problem. First, most Christians do not seek to understand the text in the

3. Ibid., 10–11.

4. Ohler, *Studying the Old Testament*, 26.

5. Ibid., 11.

historical and cultural framework of the original audience. Second, most Christians read their Bible from one basic translation and seldom compare their translation with other translations. When this happens, readers do not notice their translation of the Bible approaches the text from a different perspective than another translation.

One question Christians and non-Christians often ask is: "Why are there so many translations of the Bible today?" The reason there are so many different translations of the Bible is because translators take a different approach in translating the biblical text.[6] The purpose of these different approaches is to bring the meaning of the original text into the language of the reader. One approach to translating the biblical text is the formal correspondence approach in which the translator tries to translate the original text as literally as possible. It is an attempt at translating the original text word-for-word into English. One example of a translation that uses this approach is the American Standard Version (ASV).

Another approach is to paraphrase the original text in order to make it easy for the reader to read and understand the message of the original writer. This approach is not a full translation of the Bible. Rather, the translators take the ideas of the original writer and use modern language to convey the message the writer was presenting to his audience. The New Living Translation (NLT) and the Good News Bible (GNB) are two examples of this method.

The King James Version (KJV), the New King James Version (NKJV), and the Revised Standard Version (RSV) are translations that attempt to be faithful to the original intent of the writer. These translations seldom change the text even when the meaning of the text is not very clear. On the other hand, the New Revised Standard Version (NRSV) and the New International Version (NIV) use a dynamic equivalence approach in which the translators try to be faithful to the original text, but at times change the intent of the writers by using inclusive language and interpreting some words in order to clarify the meaning of the text for today's audience.

So, for an in-depth study of the Bible, one must select a translation that seeks to retain, as much as possible, the structure and meaning of the original text. Translations that translate the ideas of the original writer into today's way of speaking may be good for devotional reading, but they are not ideal for an in-depth study of the Bible.

---

6. A good introduction to different approaches to Bible translation is found in Sumney, *The Bible*, from which some of the material below was taken.

Introduction

The approach taken in the studies found in this book is to compare how different translations have approached difficult texts in the Old Testament. In the process of studying these texts, I look for the message of the biblical writer and seek to understand his message to the original audience. I then invite readers to reread the text in light of this new understanding of the intent of the original writer. If I succeed in motivating readers to reread the text from a different perspective, then I will have accomplished my goal of challenging readers to become better students of the Old Testament.

SECTION ONE

The Pentateuch

1

The Creation of Animals in Genesis 2:19

DURING A SEMINAR ON the Bible and evolution, the presenter tried to explain Genesis 2:19 and the creation of the animals after the creation of man. One student in the class asked a very important question: "how do you explain that in Genesis 1 the animals were created before man?" The presenter tried to explain how the creation of man and animals in Genesis 2 fits into the creation of animals and man in Genesis 1. In the process, the presenter gave the student a most unconvincing answer, an answer that did not address the issue, because it was based on a mistranslation of Genesis 2:19.

This kind of approach to Genesis 1 and 2 leaves students perplexed because the explanation creates more questions than answers. In addition, superficial explanations create doubts in the minds of educated believers who are confronted with the claims of science and the teachings of the Bible. But the presenter cannot be blamed for the unconvincing answer. Genesis 2:19 has caused problems for translators and scholars alike, and the answer of the teacher was based on a mistranslation of Genesis 2:19 found in the NIV. Below are two translations of Genesis 2:19 (the problem section of the text is in italics).

This is the translation of Genesis 2:19 in the NRSV: "So out of the ground the LORD God *formed* every animal of the field and every bird of the air, and brought them to the man to see what he would call them; and whatever the man called every living creature, that was its name."[1] The reading of the

---

1. Unless otherwise noted, all Scripture quotations are taken from the New Revised Standard Version (NRSV).

NRSV is also found in the following English translations of the Bible: ASV, HCSB, JPS, KJV, NAB, NASB, NJB, NET, NLT, RSV, and the TNK.

This is the translation of Genesis 2:19 in the NIV: "Now the LORD God *had formed* out of the ground all the wild animals and all the birds in the sky. He brought them to the man to see what he would name them; and whatever the man called each living creature, that was its name." The reading of the NIV is also found in the following English translations of the Bible: ESV, GWN, and the TNIV.

The problem with the two translations is evident. The NRSV's translation indicates that the animals were created after the creation of man in 2:7. The NIV's translation implies that the animals were already created ("Now the LORD God *had formed*") before the creation of man in Genesis 2:7. The problem with the NIV's translation is that, according to Hebrew grammar, this translation of Genesis 2:19 is unacceptable. This translation of the NIV was adopted in order to harmonize the conflict between Genesis 1 and 2.

The order of creation in Genesis 1 and 2 is different. The order of creation in Genesis 1 is: light, heavens, earth, seas, vegetation, trees, sun, moon, stars, sea monsters, fish, birds, animals, and man and woman (created together). The order of creation in Genesis 2 is: man created from the dust, the garden, trees and vegetation, animals, birds, and the woman (created from man).

How then can this difference between Genesis 1 and Genesis 2 be solved? H. C. Leupold, in his commentary on Genesis writes: "It would not, in our estimation, be wrong to translate *yatsar* as a pluperfect in this instance: 'he had molded.' The insistence of the critics upon a plain past is partly the result of the attempt to make chapters one and two clash at as many points as possible."[2]

Victor P. Hamilton, in his commentary on Genesis, writes: "Many commentators have maintained that in this verse one finds a classic illustration of a major conflict between the sequence of creation in 1:1—2:4a and that in 2:4bff. In one, (1:24–25) animals precede man. In the other, (2:19) animals come after man. It is possible to translate *formed* as 'had formed' (so NIV)."[3]

As I mentioned above, the translation of the NIV is unacceptable. John Sailhamer, in his commentary on Genesis, writes: "The NIV has offered an untenable solution in its rendering the waw consecutive in *wayyiser* by a pluperfect: 'Now the LORD God *had* formed.' Not only is such a translation

---

2. Leupold, *Exposition of Genesis*, 130.
3. Hamilton, *The Book of Genesis*, 176.

for the waw consecutive hardly possible . . . but it misses the very point of the narrative, namely, that the animals were created in response to God's declaration that it was not good that man should be alone (2:18)."[4] Franz Delitzsch, in his commentary on Genesis, made a similar argument. Delitzsch writes: "The meaning cannot be that the animals had already been created, and are now brought to be named: such a sense is excluded by grammar and misses the point of the passage."[5] Thus, as Sailhamer (and Delitzsch) points out, the translation of the NIV is wrong, and it misses the point the author is trying to make about man's loneliness. And it is out of this wrong translation that many pastors and commentators err in their interpretation of Genesis 2:19.

A better explanation of Genesis 2:19 has been proposed by U. Cassuto. In his commentary on the book of Genesis, Cassuto said the translation "had formed" cannot be considered a serious translation of Genesis 2:19. Cassuto's view is that Genesis 2:19 only mentions the creation of two kinds of animals: the animals of the field and the birds of the air.[6]

Since in Genesis 2:20 Adam names three kinds of animals—cattle, the birds of the air, and the animals of the field—Cassuto proposes that the cattle were already in the garden with the man. According to Cassuto, the animals of the field and the birds of the air had already been dispersed over all the earth. So, God formed a particular specimen of the animals of the field and the birds of the air so man could name them. Cassuto writes: "Of all the species of beasts and flying creatures that had already been created and had spread over the face of the earth and the firmament of the heavens, the LORD God now formed particular specimens for the purpose of presenting them all before man in the midst of the Garden."[7]

Cassuto's view has been adopted by both Hamilton and Sailhamer and by many other commentators. This interpretation of Genesis 2:19 solves the contradiction of the accounts of the creation of the animals in Genesis 1 and 2. It also provides a way of integrating Genesis 2 into Genesis 1. However, this interpretation is not very convincing. Cassuto's interpretation is only a supposition. He supposes the animals of the field and the birds of the air had already been dispersed over all the earth, but there is no evidence of this in the text. His view is just another attempt at harmonizing Genesis 1 and 2.

4. Sailhamer, "Genesis," 48.
5. Delitzsch, *A New Commentary on Genesis*, 67.
6. Cassuto, *Genesis*, 128–29.
7. Ibid.

It is evident that the order of creation in Genesis 1 and 2 is different and cannot be easily reconciled. The text of Genesis 1 and 2 points to two different stories of creation and no harmonizing of the text will solve the problem. The NIV's translation violates the rules of Hebrew grammar in order to present an ideological interpretation of the text.

Evangelical Christians believe in the reliability of the Bible as the word of God. As Richard F. Carlson and Tremper Longman III write in their book dealing with the issues of science, creation, and the Bible,[8] one can believe the Bible is the inspired word of God and still believe Genesis 1 and 2 are two different creation stories presenting different theological perspectives of what God did when he created the world.

8. Carlson and Longman III, *Science, Creation and the Bible.*

2

The Serpent Was Right

GENESIS 5:5 SAYS ADAM lived 930 years and then he died. The longevity of the patriarchs has been a matter of debate. The many different interpretations about the age of the patriarchs demonstrate that scholars have not yet found a good explanation for the longevity of the antediluvian population.

The statement that Adam died at the ripe old-age of 930 years is surprising in light of God's words to Adam in Genesis 2:17. After God made man and placed him in the garden of Eden, God gave Adam the following command: "You may freely eat of every tree of the garden; but of the tree of the knowledge of good and evil you shall not eat, for in the day that you eat of it you shall die" (Gen 2:16–17). When Adam told Eve of God's prohibition, he probably also told her they were forbidden even to touch the fruit of the tree, for when the serpent enticed Eve to eat of the fruit of the tree, Eve said to the serpent: "God said, 'You shall not eat of the fruit of the tree that is in the middle of the garden, nor shall you touch it, or you shall die'" (Gen 3:3). In response to Eve's reluctance to eat of the fruit, the serpent said to the woman: "You will not die; for God knows that when you eat of it your eyes will be opened, and you will be like God, knowing good and evil" (Gen 3:4–5). The serpent was right. The serpent did not lie, for everything the serpent said to Eve happened. This is what happened:

First, Eve touched the fruit (Gen 3:6) and nothing happened. Second, Eve ate the fruit and gave it to Adam who was by her side (Gen 3:6) and neither of them died. Third, Adam and Eve became like God, knowing good and evil. God himself confirmed this truth because after Adam and Eve ate of the tree, God said: "See, the man has become like one of us, knowing good and evil" (Gen 3:22).

If the serpent was right and Adam and Eve did not die when they ate from the tree of the knowledge of good and evil, what then did God mean when he told Adam that "in the day that you eat of it you shall die?" The Hebrew construction of the verb in Genesis 2:17 includes two forms of the verb מות (*mût*, "to die"): the infinitive absolute and the imperfect. In Hebrew, the infinitive absolute emphasizes an action when it immediately precedes the finite verb.

Gesenius, in his *Hebrew Grammar*, writes: "The infinitive absolute used *before* the verb to *strengthen* the verbal idea, i. e. to emphasize in this way either the certainty (especially in the case to threats) or the forcibleness and completeness of an occurrence." He translates *môt tāmût* (מוֹת תָּמוּת) *thou shalt surely die*.[1] Thus, the full implication of God's threat to Adam is clear: Adam must not eat from the tree of the knowledge of good and evil, for the moment he eats from it he would die. But Adam ate from the tree of knowledge of good and evil and he did not die. So, how must one understand God's prohibition in Genesis 2:17?

One way to interpret the divine prohibition is to say that since one day with God is like a thousand years (2 Pet 3:8), then Adam died before "the Lord's day" was over. Another way of interpreting the prohibition is by taking the infinitive form of the verb and translating it as a verbal noun: "dying you shall die." Thus, God's threat means that if Adam ate from the tree of the knowledge of good and evil, then, he would eventually die. The Septuagint translates 2:17 as "you shall die by death."

Another interpretation is that if Adam disobeyed God's command, he would become mortal. However, this interpretation contradicts Genesis because the book seems to imply that humans were already mortal. The book of Genesis says man would only live forever after eating from the tree of life: "Then the LORD God said, 'See, the man has become like one of us, knowing good and evil; and now, he might reach out his hand and take also from the tree of life, and eat, and live forever'" (Gen 3:22).

In his commentary *Genesis 1–11*, Claus Westermann notes that the expression "in the day" (Gen 2:17) has a general meaning in the Old Testament and the expression must not be understood literally, inferring death would occur immediately after the transgression. God's words to Adam, "in the day that you eat of it you shall die," according to Westermann, "is not a threat of death, but rather the clear expression of the limit which is the necessary accompaniment of the freedom entrusted to humanity in the command. To

---

1. GKC, 113n.

say no to God—and this is what freedom allows—is ultimately to say no to life; for life comes from God."[2] The divine threat should be taken literally, that Adam and Eve should have died on the day they violated the prohibition not to eat from the tree of the knowledge of good and evil.

Gordon J. Wenham's interpretation of this threat as "death before death," an interpretation that appears in his commentary on Genesis, does not explain the nature of the divine threat. He writes: "If to be expelled from the camp of Israel [as lepers were] was to 'die,' expulsion from the garden was an even more drastic kind of death. In this sense they did die on the day they ate of the tree: they were no longer able to have daily conversation with God, enjoy his bounteous provision, and eat of the tree of life; instead they had to toil for food, suffer, and eventually return to the dust from which they were taken."[3]

The reason the divine threat was not fulfilled was because the grace of God intervened and the penalty was not carried out. Probably the best commentary on this verse is found in 2 Peter 3:9: "The Lord is not slow in keeping his word, as he seems to some, but he is waiting in mercy for you, not desiring the destruction of any, but that all may be turned from their evil ways" (2 Pet 3:9 BBE).

This was the same position taken by John Skinner in his commentary on Genesis. According to Skinner, the simple explanation as to why the punishment was not carried out "is that God, having regard to the circumstances of the temptation, changed His purpose and modified the penalty."[4]

Westermann also intimates a change in God's decision to carry out the punishment. He writes: "After the man and the woman have eaten from the tree, a new situation arises in which God acts differently from the way he had indicated." God's failure to carry out the punishment "shows that God's dealing with his creatures cannot be pinned down, not even by what God has said previously."[5] Westermann concludes his study of Genesis 2:17 by saying: "And so even God's acts and words are open to misinterpretation and the serpent makes use of this."[6] It was Westermann who misinterpreted God's word to Adam when he said the words in Genesis 2:17 are not a threat, but only a warning.

2. Westermann, *Genesis 1–11*, 224.

3. Wenham, *Genesis*, 74.

4. Skinner, *Genesis*, 67.

5. Westermann, *Genesis 1–11*, 225.

6. Ibid.

The serpent did not misunderstand God. The serpent knew Eve would not die because it knew the true nature of God, that he was a compassionate God who is gracious to whom he wants to be gracious and who shows mercy on whom he wants to show mercy (Exod 33:19). As the Lord said to Moses at the time he had decided to consume Israel because of their great sin (Exod 32:10): "The LORD, the LORD, a God merciful and gracious, slow to anger, and abounding in steadfast love and faithfulness, keeping steadfast love for thousands, forgiving iniquity and transgression and sin" (Exod 34:6–7).

So, when it comes to understanding God's acts and words, Westermann was wrong and the serpent was right.

3

The Seed of the Woman

GENESIS 3:15 IS CONSIDERED by many Christians to be the first messianic prophecy of the Old Testament: "And I will put enmity between thee and the woman, and between thy seed and her seed; it shall bruise thy head, and thou shalt bruise his heel" (Gen 3:15 KJV). The Christological interpretation of this verse is accepted by most Catholics and evangelical Christians as a word of the promise in which the seed of Satan (the demons and the rebellious angels) would strike the seed of the woman, and the seed of the woman, Christ, would deliver the fatal blow by crushing the head of Satan. The eschatological interpretation of this text has become the norm in many Christian contexts and any departure of a Christological interpretation of Genesis 3:15 is considered bad exegesis. As Victor Hamilton writes in his book, "I believe that any reflection on Genesis 3:15 that fails to underscore the messianic emphasis of the verse is guilty of a serious exegetical error."[1]

In this essay I will argue against Hamilton's argument, that is, against the messianic interpretation of Genesis 3:15, and I will seek to demonstrate that an eschatological interpretation of Genesis 3:15 is not supported by a proper exegesis of the text.

Genesis 3:15 does not appear in the New Testament. However, many interpreters see the statement of Paul in Romans 16:20 as a reference to the promise of Genesis 3:15. Paul wrote: "And the God of peace shall bruise Satan under your feet shortly" (KJV). Victor Hamilton associates the promise of Genesis 3:15 with God's promises to David. He refers to God's covenant with David (2 Sam 7) in which God promised an eternal kingdom to David

1. Hamilton, *Handbook*, 51.

through David's "seed" (2 Sam 7:16). Hamilton cites Psalm 89:23 in which God promised to "crush" all those who opposed David. He also cites the fact that Jesus Christ, the seed of David, is the one "born of a woman" (Gal 4:4) who will reign "until he puts all his enemies under his feet" (1 Cor 15:25).

Hamilton gives what he considers "three phenomena" in Genesis 3:15 that reinforce the messianic interpretation of the text.[2] First, the Hebrew masculine word for seed occurs with a third person feminine pronominal suffix, which then is translated as "her seed." To Hamilton, this construction is unique and important. He writes: "The uniqueness of the construction becomes even more apparent in the Septuagint with its reference to the woman's sperm—'her sperm(a)'! (where is the man, the father?)."[3]

Second, Hamilton appeals to the Septuagint, the Greek translation of the Old Testament, to confirm his interpretation. The Septuagint uses the third person masculine pronoun "he" to modify the word "seed," which in Greek is neuter in gender. The Septuagint could have used "it" to refer to "seed," but by using "he," the translators of the Septuagint had in mind one individual, not many individuals.

Third, Hamilton emphasizes that the confrontation between the woman and the serpent is not an accident of history, but something God himself initiated. Hamilton writes, "It is an event as foreordained as the incarnation of Jesus."[4]

To properly understand the problems translators of the Bible face when translating Genesis 3:15, it becomes necessary to compare grammatical rules between English and Hebrew. In Hebrew, there are only two genders. Everything is either masculine or feminine. In English, there are three genders, masculine, feminine, and neuter. For instance, in Hebrew, the name of a city is feminine. In English, the name of a city is neuter. In Hebrew, Jerusalem is a "she." In English, Chicago is an "it."

This is how the lexicon defines the Hebrew word זֶרַע (zera'), the word translated "seed" in English: "noun, masculine."[5] This means the word will have a masculine pronoun "he" since the word in Hebrew is a masculine word. Most of the time in the Hebrew Bible the word "seed" has a collective sense. When it refers to plants, the word means the seed of trees or the seed of fruits. At the time of creation, God said: "Let the earth put forth vegetation,

2. Ibid., 50–51.

3. Ibid., 50.

4. Ibid., 51.

5. BDB, 282.

plants yielding seed, and fruit trees bearing fruit in which is their seed, each according to its kind, upon the earth" (Gen 1:11). When the word is used of people, it generally means offspring or descendants. When Eli blessed El-kanah and his wife Hannah, he said: "May the LORD give you children by this woman (1 Sam 2:20 RSV). The KJV translates the same verse as follows: "The LORD give thee seed of this woman."

The word also can be used to refer to an individual. The son of Hagar is called "your seed": "I will multiply thy seed exceedingly that it shall not be numbered for multitude" (Gen 16:10 KJV). But the same word can also have a collective meaning: "I will increase your descendants so much that they will be too numerous to count" (Gen 16:10 NIV).

The same collective idea appears in God's promise to Abraham in Genesis 12:7:

KJV: "Unto thy seed will I give this land."

ESV: "To your offspring I will give this land."

RSV: "To your descendants I will give this land."

NJB: "I shall give this country to your progeny."

The word "seed" is used with a double meaning in Genesis 3:15. The word refers to the descendants of the woman ("her seed") and to the off-spring of the serpent ("your seed"). The problem with translating Genesis 3:15 is that the translators tend to introduce their theological views into the text and then translate the verse accordingly. A few examples will suffice.

The translators of the KJV had an ambivalent understanding of the word "seed": "And I will put enmity between thee and the woman, and be-tween thy seed and her seed; it shall bruise thy head, and thou shalt bruise his heel." Here the translators used the word "it" to refer to the seed of the woman, but then they used the expression "his heel" to refer to the seed of the woman as a person.

The translators of the NASB infused a Christological understanding to the word "seed" in their translation of Genesis 3:15: "And I will put enmity between you and the woman, And between your seed and her seed; He shall bruise you on the head, And you shall bruise him on the heel." By using the word "He" with a capital H after a semicolon, the translators of the NASB were declaring that the verse was referring to the work of Christ. The translators of the HCSB have the same view, but their translation is ambivalent since they use "He" with a capital H after a period: "I will put hostility between you and the woman, and between your seed and her seed. He will strike your head, and you will strike his heel."

The translators of the DRA, a Catholic translation of the Latin Vulgate, translated Genesis 3:15 from a Mariological perspective: "I will put enmities between thee and the woman, and thy seed and her seed: she shall crush thy head, and thou shalt lie in wait for her heel." According to Mariological theology, it is Mary who crushes the head of the serpent. This translation follows Catholic exegesis, which calls these words of Genesis "The Protoevangelium," that is, the first gospel, or the first announcement of the coming Messiah.

According to Catholic theology, in the promise of Genesis 3:15 the woman is placed first to indicate the enmity is between the serpent and the woman. Thus, according to this theological perspective, the announcement of a coming Redeemer makes the woman the first enemy of Satan.

The Hebrew word זֶרַע (*zera'*) in Genesis 3:15 should be understood as a collective word with a plural meaning. The verse is referring to the descendants of the woman as well as the descendants of the serpent. This is how the Common English Bible translates Genesis 3:15: "I will put contempt between you and the woman, between your offspring and hers. They will strike your head, but you will strike at their heels." The same view was taken by the TNK, the translation of the Hebrew Bible published by The Jewish Publication Society. It reads: "I will put enmity between you and the woman, and between your offspring and hers; they shall strike at your head, and you shall strike at their heel" (Gen 3:15).

The words of Genesis 3:15 occur in the context of God's judgment and speak of the hostility between human beings and the serpent. This hostility was decreed by God as the consequence of what the serpent did in deceiving the woman. In light of the proper exegesis of the text, Gerhard von Rad writes: "The exegesis of the early church which found a messianic prophecy here, a reference to a final victory of the woman's seed (Protoevangelium), does not agree with the sense of [the] passage, quite apart from the fact that the word 'seed' may not be construed personally but only quite generally with the meaning of 'posterity.'"[6]

In his commentary on Genesis, Gordon J. Wenham understands the word "seed" to refer to "the human race."[7] Wenham writes: "While a messianic interpretation may be justified in the light of subsequent revelation

---

6. Von Rad, *Genesis*, 90.

7. Wenham, *Genesis*, 79.

. . . it would perhaps be wrong to suggest that this was the narrator's own understanding. Probably he just looked for mankind eventually to defeat the serpent's seed, the power of evil."[8] Even the ethical meaning, that the serpent represents Satan and the powers of evil, does not reflect the plain meaning of the text, which presents the serpent as a real animal, one of the wild animals that God had made (Gen 3:1).

The New Testament identifies the serpent of Genesis with Satan and the Devil: "And the great dragon was cast down, the old serpent, he that is called the Devil and Satan, the deceiver of the whole world; he was cast down to the earth, and his angels were cast down with him" (Rev 12:9 ASV). This understanding of Genesis 3:15 is not found in the Old Testament. An intimation of this idea is found in the apocryphal book, the Wisdom of Solomon: "Through the devil's envy death entered the world, and those who belong to his party experience it" (Wis 2:24 RSV).

A messianic interpretation of Genesis 3:15 is also found in the *Targum Pseudo-Jonathan*. It reads: "And I will put enmity between thee and the woman, and between the seed of thy son, and the seed of her sons; and it shall be when the sons of the woman keep the commandments of the law, they will be prepared to smite thee upon thy head; but when they forsake the commandments of the law, thou wilt be ready to wound them in their heel. Nevertheless for them there shall be a medicine, but for thee there will be no medicine; and they shall make a remedy for the heel in the days of the King Meshiha."

But, how about Hamilton's claim, a claim used by many preachers, that the Septuagint speaks of the woman's sperm, which is, according to some interpreters, a reference to the virgin birth of Christ. Since a woman receives sperm from man to conceive a child, then the woman's sperm mentioned in Genesis 3:15 must be a reference to the Holy Spirit "overshadowing" Mary (Luke 1:35).

What Hamilton does not say in his book is that the Hebrew Bible does not use the word "sperm" but "seed." "Sperm" is a Greek translation of the Hebrew word "seed." In addition, the Septuagint also has the same word, *sperma*, for the serpent. The Septuagint speaks of the *spermatos* of the woman and the *spermatos* of the serpent.

Although the messianic interpretation of Genesis 3:15 is very attractive and has served as the foundational text for many good sermons, this interpretation should be abandoned because it does not reflect a proper

8. Ibid., 81.

interpretation of the text. The translation of the Common English Bible and the translation of the Tanak is the proper way of understanding the word "seed." The Hebrew word for "seed" in Genesis 3:15 should be understood in the sense of "descendants" or "offspring."

4

Were They Really Giants?

Translating the Bible from Hebrew into English is not easy. Translators face the challenge of translating from Hebrew words and expressions that may not be similar to words and expressions in English. In addition, there are verses in the Bible where the meaning of words is known, but translators do not know what the original writer was trying to communicate. Genesis 6:4 is one of those enigmatic verses that is hard to translate because translators do not understand the original intent of the writer.

The KJV translates Genesis 6:4 as follows: "There were giants in the earth in those days; and also after that, when the sons of God came in unto the daughters of men, and they bare children to them, the same became mighty men which were of old, men of renown." The word translated "giant" in the KJV is based on the Septuagint, the translation of the Old Testament into Greek. This translation is followed by the DBY, the DRA, the GBV, the NKJV, the NLT, and the RWB.

The ESV translates: "The Nephilim were on the earth in those days, and also afterward, when the sons of God came in to the daughters of man and they bore children to them. These were the mighty men who were of old, the men of renown."

The ESV leaves the Hebrew word *Nephilim* untranslated. This procedure has been adopted by most modern translations, including the ASV, the JPS version, the NAB, the NASB, the NIV, the NJB, the NRSV, and the TNK.

The KJV uses the word "giant" to translate the word "Nephilim" in Genesis 6:4 and in Numbers 13:33. In addition, the KJV uses the word "giants" several other times, but most of them to translate the Hebrew word גִּבּוֹר (*gibbôr*, "warrior") as in Job 16:14, the word רְפָאִים (*repha'îm*, "Rephaim") or רָפָה

(*rāphāh*, "Raphah") as in 2 Sam 21:22 (the NIV uses the word "Rapha."). The Rephaim were another group of tall people who inhabited the land of Canaan before the time of the Exodus (Gen 15:20). Rephaim is a plural word in Hebrew. The NIV uses Rephaites to express the plural sense in English (Deut 2:11, 20). There were several groups of people who were called giants in the Old Testament. One of them was the Anakim. The Anakim were associated with the southern part of Canaan, especially the city of Hebron. They were a tall group of people who lived in Canaan (Deut 2:21). The word *'anāq* in Hebrew means "long-neck" or giants. The Anakim were not the only group of tall people who lived in the land of the Bible.

The Rephaim, whom the Ammonites called Zamzummites, lived in the territory of the Ammonites and were as tall as the Anakim (Deut 2:20–21). The Emim, who lived in the territory of the Moabites also were as tall as the Anakim (Deut 2:10). Both the Emim and the Anakim were considered to be Rephaim (Deut 2:11). This identification of the Rephaim with the Anakim and of the Emim with the Anakim and with the Rephaim reflects the popular view that all the inhabitants of the land were giants (Num 13:33 [H 13:34]).

When Moses sent the twelve spies to visit the land of Canaan, they identified the offspring of the Anakim with the Nephilim of Genesis 6:4 (Num 13:33). The identification of the Nephilim with the Anakim is difficult because the most important passage where the word "Nephilim" appears (Gen 6:1–4) is obscure and has produced numerous, and at times contradictory, interpretations.

Most scholars today derive the Hebrew word *Nephilim* from the Hebrew verb *nāphal*, which means "fallen ones." This is the translation adopted by the YLT: "The fallen ones were in the earth in those days, and even afterwards when sons of God come in unto daughters of men, and they have borne to them—they are the heroes, who, from of old, are the men of name."

Thus, some scholars view the Nephilim as the ones fallen from heaven, that is, divine beings or angels. Others have identified the Nephilim with robbers and people who preyed upon individuals, violent men who fell upon their victims. Some scholars have derived Nephilim from a Hebrew word *nēphel*, which means "miscarriage." These scholars understand the Nephilim as unnaturally begotten superhuman beings emerging from miscarriages.

Which translation is better? Those who translate "Nephilim" as "giants" base their translation on the statement of Genesis 6:4, which declares the Nephilim were on the earth before the flood "and also afterward." This editorial comment, "and also afterward," added by the writer of the narrative, seems to imply the Nephilim survived the flood, thus helping the writer of the biblical text identify the Nephilim with the tall people who lived in Canaan. However, the identification of the Nephilim with giants fails to deal with the moral issues raised by the commingling of "the sons of God" with "the daughters of men."

Those who leave the word "Nephilim" untranslated recognize that the meaning of the word is unclear, that the Nephilim of Genesis 6:4 were not the Anakim of Numbers 13:33, and that no translation is acceptable since the context is unclear. The best way to solve this problem of translation is to leave the word Nephilim untranslated, as the ESV and other translations have done. This solution, however, creates a huge problem because it puts the burden of interpretation on the reader. And since the average reader of the Bible does not know Hebrew and has no idea what a Nephilim is, this solution creates another problem.

The decision to leave the word "Nephilim" untranslated creates a big problem for pastors. Members of the congregation may ask their pastors: "pastor, who were the Nephilim?" When this question is asked, pastors will need to go to their library, do some research, and find the correct answer. Any question that stimulates study is a good question.

5

"As Far as Dan" (Gen 14:14)

THE NARRATIVE IN GENESIS 14 describing Abraham's struggles with the four kings from the east has generated much discussion among scholars. In Genesis 14 Abraham is portrayed not just as a lonely man sojourning through the land of Canaan, but rather as the chief of a clan, a man with a large entourage, one who is strong enough to challenge the four kings and defeat them (Gen 14:14–17).

According to the story, Lot, Abraham's nephew, was captured by the four kings from the east at the time they invaded Canaan. Lot was taken captive after the invaders sacked the land and returned back to their countries through North Syria. In order to rescue Lot, Abraham prepared a contingency of 318 men, all of them servants born in his house, and pursued the four kings "as far as Dan" (Gen 14:14) and rescued Lot, the women, the men who were taken captive, and Lot's possessions.

The purpose of this chapter is not to discuss the identity of the four kings, or the composition of chapter 14, nor the relationship between Genesis 14 and the Abraham cycle. Rather, the intent of this chapter is to discuss the meaning of the expression "as far as Dan" in Genesis 14:14.

As it stands in the text, the use of Dan is an anachronism. Dan was the fifth son of Jacob and the first son of Bilhah, the maid given by Rachel to be Jacob's secondary wife (Gen 30:6). Later on, when the people of Israel conquered the land of Canaan in the days of Joshua, the tribe of Dan received a portion of the land as its inheritance.

When Dan received its inheritance in Canaan, Dan's territory was between the tribes of Ephraim and Judah. In the days of the judges, the Amorites forced the Danites into the hill country (Judg 1:34). Later on, during the struggle between Israel and the Philistines, the Danites were oppressed by the Philistines. Shamgar, the son of Anath, killed 600 Philistines with an oxgoad and delivered Israel (Judg 3:31).

In the days of Samson, the Israelites struggled again against the Philistines, but Samson, a judge from the tribe of Dan, was not able to deliver the Danites from the oppression of the Philistines and the Danites were forced to move (Judg 18:1–31). The migration of the Danites is also mentioned in Joshua 19:47–48.

The tribe of Dan conquered Laish (Judg 18:7) and burned the city (the city is named Leshem in Josh 19:47). Then, they rebuilt the city and called it Dan. Laish was a city at the northernmost end of the land of Canaan. Eventually, the expression "from Dan to Beer-sheba" (1 Sam 3:20) came to express the northern and the southern borders of Israel. The reference to Sidon in Judges 18:28 may indicate that, at the time the Danites conquered the city, Laish was a colony of Sidon.

Thus, it is clear then that the appearance of Dan in Genesis 14:14 is an anachronism, since in the days of Abraham Dan was not yet born and there was no Dan to give name to a city located in the northern part of Canaan. The expression "as far as Dan" is also an anachronism because Moses could not have written about the location of Dan since the land of Canaan had not yet been occupied by the Israelite tribes who were living in Egypt.

The issue with this anachronism has to do with the question of Mosaic authorship of the Pentateuch. For those who accept Mosaic authorship of the Pentateuch, the anachronism of Genesis 14:14 poses a problem. Several solutions have been proposed to solve the anachronism and thus hold to the integrity of the text and to Mosaic authorship.

One proposed solution is the view that the Dan of Genesis 14:14 is not the Laish conquered by the Danites and then later renamed Dan, but that this Dan was Dan-jaan, a city mentioned in 2 Samuel 24:6. According to this view, the Dan of Genesis 14:14 belonged to Gilead (see Deut 34:1), and is no doubt the same as the Dan-jaan mentioned in 2 Samuel 24:6 in connection with Gilead.

This view should be rejected for two reasons: First, Josephus mentioned that this Dan was located near one of the sources of the Jordan.[1] In addition, the Samaritan Pentateuch, the Septuagint, and the Targum Onkelos follow the Masoretic Text. Second, many scholars believe that Dan-jaan and Dan were the same city. This view reflects the possibility that

---

1. Josephus, *Ant.* 1:10.

the scribes did not preserve the correct name of this city. Some Bible translations accept the identification of Dan-jaan with Dan.

The following translations translate "Dan" in 2 Samuel 24:6: ESV, RSV, NRSV, TNK, BBE, DRA, NAB, and the NJB. The following translations translate "Dan-jaan": KJV, NIV, NKJV, NLT, HCSB, DBY, GBV, JPS, RWB, and the YLT.

Another proposal to deal with the anachronism is the view that Dan was the original name of the city, which was renamed Laish by the Sidonians after they conquered the city. Thus, when Abraham pursued the Mesopotamian kings, he went as far as Dan, a city that already existed in the days of the patriarchs. Other scholars believe that the name Dan in Genesis 14:14 was substituted by an editor or a redactor for its older name Laish in order to reflect the new name of the city. Some scholars have identified "Jaan" with Ijon, a city located north of Dan (1 Kgs 15:20). Others have identified Dan-jaan with Denyen, one of the groups that settled in Canaan at the time of the migration of the Sea Peoples.

These explanations do not solve the anachronism in Genesis 14:14. Thus, it is clear that someone other than Moses wrote Genesis 14:14. The attempts at explaining the anachronism and at the same time defending Mosaic authorship have not been successful. The book of Genesis is an anonymous book. The Bible never says Moses wrote Genesis. It was Jewish tradition that attributed Mosaic authorship to the Pentateuch and Christians have adopted this tradition as a matter of fact. Evangelical Christians can still believe in the reliability of the Bible even if someone other than Moses wrote Genesis 14:14.

6

Abraham and the Promises of God

THE CALL OF ABRAHAM is the beginning of the story of Israel and people of faith everywhere. Abraham left a legacy that touches all believers today, becoming a model for people living as sojourners in a foreign land. Abraham's legacy as a model of a believer living as a sojourner in a foreign land is based in part on God's promise to Abraham. At the time God called Abraham, God told Abraham to leave his country, his people and his father's household and go to the land he would show him (Gen 12:1). Abraham left Haran and came to Canaan at the call of God. When Abraham came to Canaan, he "traveled through the land" (Gen 12:6). In Shechem God promised Abraham: "To your offspring I will give this land" (Gen 12:7). The descendants of Abraham would be the heirs of what God had promised to him, but the promise was made to Abraham: he would receive the land. More than once God promised that he would give the land to Abraham himself:

"All the land that you see I will give to you and your offspring forever" (Gen 13:15).

"Rise up, walk through the length and the breadth of the land, for I will give it to you" (Gen 13:17).

"He also said to him, 'I am the Lord, who brought you out of Ur of the Chaldeans to give you this land to take possession of it'" (Gen 15:7 HCSB).

"The whole land of Canaan, where you are now an alien, I will give as an everlasting possession to you and your descendants after you; and I will be their God" (Gen 17:8).

God's promise to Abraham was renewed to Isaac. At the time of the famine in Canaan, God told Isaac not to go to Egypt, and then made him this promise: "Stay in this land for a while, and I will be with you and will bless you. For to you and your descendants I will give all these lands and will confirm the oath I swore to your father Abraham" (Gen 26:3). The promise to Isaac was that God would give to him, Isaac, and to his descendants, the land God promised to give to Abraham.

Then, the same promise was made to Jacob. At the time Jacob was fleeing from his brother Esau, God appeared to Jacob in a vision and promised to give him the land of Canaan. The Lord spoke to Jacob and said: "I am the Lord, the God of your father Abraham and the God of Isaac. I will give you and your descendants the land on which you are lying" (Gen 28:13). Each of the patriarchs received a promise from God that they, Abraham, Isaac, and Jacob, would receive the land in which they lived. Throughout their lives, the patriarchs lived as sojourners in the land God promised to give to them. Abraham "traveled through the land," "pitched his tent" here and there, moved from one place to another, walking through the length and breadth of the land as if claiming the land God had given to him.

Some Christians believe Abraham died before seeing the fulfillment of God's promise of the land of Canaan. Abraham spent most of his life moving around the land of Canaan living as a stranger in a strange land, but it was for later generations to experience the gift of the land. However, if Abraham died before receiving the land, what then of God's promise? God promised Abraham: "Go, walk through the length and breadth of the land, for I am giving it to you" (Gen 13:17). And how about God's promise to Isaac and Jacob that they too would receive the land? Did the patriarchs die without receiving God's promise?

There is, however, another way of understanding the fulfillment of the promise God made to the patriarchs. When Sarah died in Hebron, Abraham bought a parcel of land in Canaan (Gen 23). In his dealings with the owners of the land, Abraham bought a cave in which to bury Sarah and a large field with many trees on it.

When looked at from the perspective of God's promise to Abraham, the purchase of the cave of Machpelah is very significant. The writer of Genesis is emphasizing that Abraham became the owner of a portion of the land of Canaan legally, the same land that one day would belong to his descendants. In fact, the plot of land became the final resting place for the patriarchs and their wives. On the land Abraham bought to bury Sarah, he was buried. In addition, Isaac and Rebecca, Jacob and Leah were also buried there (Gen 49:29–32). John Goldingay writes: "Abraham and Sarah do come into secure legal possession of land in Canaan, even if it is a burial possession. . . . It is a mere foothold, or rather skeleton-hold, in the land, but it means that Sarah, and in due course Abraham, Isaac, Rebekah, Leah and Jacob, will be able to rest there forever in the land Yhwh promised."[1]

God's promise to give Abraham the land of Canaan raises a question: can God's promises be trusted? The narrative about Sarah's death fits well within the perspective of God's covenant with Abraham. Gerhard von Rad, in his commentary on Genesis writes: "Did the patriarchs who forsook everything for the sake of the promise go unrewarded? No, answers our narrative. In death they were heirs and no longer 'strangers.' A very small part of the Promised Land, the grave, belonged to them."[2]

The writer of Genesis is showing that Abraham came into possession of the land as a gift from God, as evidence that God's promise was already being fulfilled in the days of Abraham. In the New Testament, Paul says the presence of the Holy Spirit in the hearts of believers is a "deposit, guaranteeing what is to come" (2 Cor 1:22). In death, the patriarchs received a portion of the land and that burial ground became a deposit, guaranteeing what was to come.

---

1. Goldingay, *Old Testament Theology*, 1:232–33.
2. Von Rad, *Genesis*, 245.

7

The Sacrifice of Isaac

PREACHING GOOD AND EFFECTIVE sermons from the Old Testament requires hard work. In preparing their sermons, ministers must read good commentaries, consult different translations, and use the best scholarship available to them in order to gain a better understanding of the biblical text. A biblical sermon is the proclamation of God's truth, thus, before preaching from any text, ministers must go through the most rigorous study of the text in order to understand the historical and cultural backgrounds of the passage they are using, as well as the precise meaning of the words used in the text. The success of a good sermon depends on the proper interpretation of the text. When interpreting a text, the minister must look at the historical context of the passage and the language used by the writer. The most pressing issue faced by those who preach from the Old Testament is how to interpret the message of a text that was written centuries ago in such a way that it becomes relevant to people living in the twenty-first century.

There are many ways of preaching from the Old Testament. One way to make the Old Testament relevant for people today is to interpret it in the light of the complete work of Jesus Christ. Often, this method of interpretation requires the spiritualization of a biblical passage at the expense of the grammatical-historical sense of the text. The spiritualization of the Old Testament degrades the historical value of the text and brings into the text a secondary meaning that was not present in the original intent of the writer or is not present in the actual reading of the text.

Some preachers devalue the text of the Old Testament by adding meaning to words and events in order to produce a developed doctrine of the teachings of the New Testament. Bernard Ramm, in his book *Protestant*

Biblical Interpretation, said that, "allegorists might find something far richer about Jesus Christ and salvation in Genesis than in Luke."[1] Take for instance the story of the sacrifice of Isaac in Genesis 22. At the command of God, Abraham took his beloved son Isaac to sacrifice him on the top of a mountain the Lord had chosen. God's request evoked deep feelings in Abraham, and yet, contrary to human desires, Abraham obeyed the divine command, took his son, and prepared to do what God had demanded of him. As Abraham and Isaac walked to the designated place, Isaac sensing something was missing, asked his father: "Behold the fire and the wood: but where is the lamb for a burnt offering?" (Gen 22:7 KJV). Abraham's answer to Isaac is a declaration of faith and confidence in God. Abraham said to his son: "My son, God will provide himself a lamb for a burnt offering" (Gen 22:8 KJV). Abraham's reply does not answer Isaac's question. As Walter Brueggemann says in his commentary on Genesis: "Abraham does not tell Isaac all he wants to know because Abraham himself does not know."[2]

The translation of verse 8 as it appears in the KJV is not very clear. As the KJV translates the Hebrew text of verse 8, it seems God will provide himself as the lamb for the sacrifice. And this is how M. R. DeHaan understood the verse. In his book, DeHaan writes: "Notice it does not say 'God will himself provide a lamb,' but it says, 'God will provide *himself*' [emphasis his]. Translated freely Abraham says God Himself is going to be the Lamb of sacrifice."[3]

The problem with the reading of the KJV is that in translating verse 8, the translators of the KJV did not translate a preposition ("for") and a definite article ("the") that are present in the Hebrew text. If the translators of the KJV had paid attention to these minor details, the translation would read like this: "God will provide for himself the lamb for a burnt offering" (Gen 22:8 ESV).

The translation of Genesis 22:8 in the ESV is much superior to the translation of the KJV. Had DeHaan used the ESV, he would have no grounds to preach that God was providing himself as the sacrificial lamb. There is no doubt DeHaan's sermon was a blessing and inspired many people who heard that interpretation of Genesis 22:8. But just because a sermon is inspiring and even life changing, it does not mean the sermon is true to the real meaning of the text. The writer of Genesis 22:8 never intended to say God would offer himself as a sacrificial lamb. It is only a

1. Ramm, *Protestant Biblical Interpretation*, 50.
2. Brueggemann, *Genesis*, 188.
3. DeHaan, *Portraits of Christ in Genesis*, 139.

poor interpretation of a flawed translation that can produce a sermon that completely misunderstands the original meaning of the biblical writer.

There are three lessons every preacher must learn in the preparation of sermons. First, it is important to check the original languages to ascertain whether a translation is close to the original meaning of the text. Second, since most preachers cannot read Hebrew and Greek, it becomes imperative that preachers consult more than one translation in the preparation of their sermons and compare how different translations translate the text being used as the basis for the sermon. The third lesson preachers must learn is this: there is no substitute for personal study and hard work. Proclaiming God's word to a congregation is a great responsibility. Preachers must work hard to make sure the message they preach was given to them by God and reflects the truth of the text.

8

The Rape of Bilhah

A SAD AND DEMORALIZING story about Jacob's family occurs in Genesis 35:22. The text says: "While Israel lived in that land, Reuben went and lay with Bilhah his father's concubine; and Israel heard of it. Now the sons of Jacob were twelve." Bilhah was the handmaid of Rachel, the servant whom Laban, Rachel's father, gave to her at the occasion of Rachel's marriage to Jacob (Gen 29:29). When Rachel realized she was unable to give a son to Jacob, she gave her handmaid to her husband so they might obtain children through her servant. Rachel said to Jacob: "Here is my maid Bilhah; go in to her, that she may bear upon my knees and that I too may have children through her." Out of this arrangement, Bilhah gave Jacob two sons and became the mother of Dan and Naphtali (Gen 30:3–8).

Such a practice was common in the ancient Near East. The Nuzi tablets reveal that if a wife was childless she could provide her husband with a slave who would then become his concubine.[1] When a son was born out of this union, the child would be adopted by the mistress of the slave woman as her own son. Bilhah then was Jacob's secondary wife. After Rachel died (Gen 35:19), Jacob moved to Migdal Eder (Gen 35:21), a place probably within the territory of Judah (Josh 15:21). After Jacob had settled down in that place, Reuben, Jacob's firstborn, slept with Bilhah, Jacob's secondary wife (Gen 35:22). Because of his transgression, Reuben lost the privileges accorded to the firstborn son. In the blessings of his children, Jacob said to Reuben: "Reuben, you are my firstborn, my might and the first fruits of my vigor, excelling in rank and excelling in power. Unstable as water, you

---

1. Bright, *History of Israel*, 79.

shall no longer excel because you went up onto your father's bed; then you defiled it—you went up onto my couch" (Gen 49:3–4).

Reuben's rape of Jacob's concubine is a tragic event in the history of Jacob's family, a family that had experienced many other tragic incidents. It is interesting that the text says Jacob "heard of it," but does not say what Jacob did or said to Reuben in response to what his son had done. That Jacob did or said something to Reuben is implied in the Hebrew text. Most readers of Genesis 35:22 in the English versions of this verse do not notice a strange construction in the Hebrew text. In the Hebrew text of Genesis 35:22 that appears in the *Biblia Hebraica Stuttgartensia*, the verse has two sets of accents. The two *sillûqs* in the verse show that in antiquity, there were two different divisions of verse 22 (a *sillûq* is a Hebrew accent that marks the end of a verse in the Hebrew Bible).

The Eastern tradition regarded Genesis 35:22 as two verses and the Western tradition regarded it as one verse. This means the first *sillûq* that appears at the end of "Israel" ("... and heard Israel") indicates the first ending of the verse (the Eastern tradition). The second *sillûq* at the end of "twelve" is the second verse in the Eastern tradition, but it marks the end of verse 22 in the Western tradition. The verse division of the Eastern tradition is confirmed by the number of verses listed in the Masorah of Genesis. In *Parashah* 8 (Gen 32:4—36:43)[2] the Masorah says the *Parashah* has a total of 154 verses (the Eastern tradition). However, there are only 153 verses in Genesis 32:4—36:43 (the Western tradition). In his explanation of the double accent, Gesenius writes that the double accentuation "intended for public reading, aims at uniting vv. 22 and 23 into one, so as to pass rapidly over the unpleasant statement in v. 22."[3]

By leaving a gap between two sections of verse 22, the writer of Genesis was indicating that some of the text has been either lost or deliberately deleted. It is also possible Jacob did or said something to his son, but unfortunately, we will never know Jacob's reaction since the details are missing from the text.

In order to protect the reputation of Jacob and Reuben, the *Targum Pseudo-Jonathan* changes the text by saying that no incest occurred:

> And it was while Israel dwelt in this land that Reuben went and confounded the bed of Bilhah the concubine of his father, which had been ordained along with the bed of Leah his mother; and this

2. A *Parashah* is a section of the Torah read on the Sabbath in the synagogue.
3. GKC, 15p.

is reputed with regard to him, as if he had lain with her. And Israel heard it, and it afflicted him, and he said, alas, that one should have come forth from me so profane, even as Ishmael came forth from Abraham, and Esau from my father! The Spirit of Holiness answered and thus spake to him: fear not, for all are righteous and none of them is profane! So, after Benjamin was born, the sons of Jakob were twelve" (Gen 35:22 *Tg. Ps.-J.*).

The Talmud (*b. Šabb.* 55b) also seeks to absolve Reuben of incest:

R. Samuel b. Nahman said in R. Jonathan's name: Whoever maintains that Reuben sinned is merely making an error, for it is said, Now the sons of Jacob were twelve, teaching that they were all equal. Then how do I interpret, and he lay with Bilhah his father's concubine? This teaches that he transposed his father's couch, and the Writ imputes [blame] to him as though he had lain with her. It was taught, R. Simeon b. Eleazar said: That righteous man was saved from that sin and that deed did not come to his hand.

Notwithstanding Rabbinic effort to absolve Reuben of incest, the words of Jacob to Reuben in Genesis 49:3–4 clearly show Reuben violated his father's marriage bed. Later Israelite laws strongly condemned the kind of incest committed by Reuben: "You shall not uncover the nakedness of your father's wife; it is the nakedness of your father" (Lev 18:8). In addition, Leviticus 20:11 says that any man who sleeps with his father's wife shall be put to death. Deuteronomy 27:20 says "The one who sleeps with his father's wife is cursed, for he has violated his father's marriage bed."

9

Miriam, a Leader in Israel

FEMINIST HERMENEUTICS HAS MADE an impact on biblical scholarship because it has demonstrated to interpreters that the biblical text reflects the patriarchal views of the society that gave birth to the text. In addition, feminist interpreters have shown that some of these same patriarchal values and concerns have affected biblical translations. Feminist writers like to emphasize that the stories in the Bible were written by men for men. In many stories about women in the Old Testament, women remain nameless, as in the case of Jephthah's daughter and the concubine who was raped and then dismembered, or they remain voiceless, their voices only being heard through the voice of the male redactor.

The portrayal of Miriam in the biblical text may demonstrate how the biblical writers lessened her influence as one of the leaders of the Israel-ite community at the time Israel journeyed through the wilderness. The purpose of this study is to look at Miriam and how she is portrayed in the biblical text and then focus on Micah 6:4 and how the NIV portrays Miriam in its translation of that text. Miriam appears in five books of the Old Testament: Exodus, Numbers, Deuteronomy, 1 Chronicles, and Micah. Her name appears fifteen times in these books, but only thirteen in the NIV. On two occasions, in Numbers 12:10 and 12:15, the NIV uses the pronoun "she" instead of using Miriam's name, as do most translations.

In Miriam's first appearance in the biblical text, she is the nameless sister of Moses who watches him on the waters of the Nile. She is called only "his sister" (Exod 2:4). In this text the reader can see the initiatives taken by Miriam: Miriam speaks to Pharaoh's daughter and offers to find someone to take care of the child. Because of her, Moses lived his formative years with his own mother. Because of Miriam, Moses lives and does not die. Miriam saves her brother before he can save a single Hebrew.

In Exodus 15:20, Miriam is called הַנְּבִיאָה (*hanebîʾāh*, "the prophetess"). A prophet (נָבִיא, *nābîʾ*) is a person called by God. Miriam was called by God to lead the people together with Moses and Aaron. Miriam was assigned a prophetical role because she led the community in celebrating God's victory over the Egyptian army: "Sing to the LORD, for he has triumphed gloriously; the horse and his rider he has thrown into the sea" (Exod 15:21).

And yet, the song of Miriam has been attributed to Moses: "Then Moses and the people of Israel sang this song to the LORD, saying, 'I will sing to the LORD, for he has triumphed gloriously; the horse and his rider he has thrown into the sea'" (Exod 15:1). Some scholars have proposed that Miriam's song was a response to Moses' song. However, a critical review of Moses' song in Exodus 15 reveals that the song was written many years after the event. Miriam's song may be an old composition celebrating Israel's crossing the sea. Moses received the credit for the song, but it was Miriam who led Israel in celebrating God's victory.

In Numbers 12:1–15 there is a controversy over the issue of leadership. In Numbers 12:2, Aaron and Miriam asked Moses: "Has the LORD indeed spoken only through Moses? Has he not spoken through us also?" (Num 12:12). However, Numbers 12:1 attributes the controversy to questions about Moses' Cushite wife. The text is not clear on the nature of the conflict, but it seems Miriam was raising an issue that reflected a concern in the community. Although both Aaron and Miriam are involved in this controversy, only Miriam was punished as a result of this challenge to Moses' leadership. The public nature of her punishment may indicate the issue was of interest to the whole community.

That Miriam was a leader in Israel is clearly seen in Micah 6:4: "For I brought you up from the land of Egypt and redeemed you from the house of slavery, and I sent before you Moses, Aaron, and Miriam" (Mic 6:4 ESV). In this text Miriam is named as one of the leaders of Israel, together with Moses and Aaron, whom God sent to lead the people out of Egypt. The prophet Micah lists Moses, Aaron, and Miriam as the three leaders of Israel. Thus, Micah's statement reflects an ancient tradition that affirms that Miriam had a very significant leadership role in early Israelite history, a role that in later writing was downgraded partly in order to promote Moses as the prominent leader of Israel. Although the biblical text refers to Moses and Aaron as the leaders of the community, the text in Micah 6:4 reveals Miriam was their equal.

Anderson and Freeman acknowledge the importance of Micah's statement. They write: "What makes Micah's simple statement so remarkable, and so puzzling, is the fact that nowhere in the tradition are the three siblings presented in a shared leadership role."[1] However, the NIV translation of Micah 6:4 looks like an attempt to diminish Miriam as a leader in Israel. The NIV translates: "I brought you up out of Egypt and redeemed you from the land of slavery. I sent Moses to lead you, also Aaron and Miriam" (Mic 6:4 NIV). The same translation is found in the TNIV. The translation of the NIV does not reflect the biblical text. All the other translations of Micah 6:4 reflect the Hebrew text: "For I brought you up from the land of Egypt and redeemed you from the house of slavery, and I sent before you Moses, Aaron, and Miriam" (Mic 6:4 ESV).

The translation of the NIV takes away the unique leadership role Miriam had in the community. By separating Aaron and Miriam from Moses, the NIV elevates Moses' position ("I sent Moses to lead you") and diminishes Miriam almost to an afterthought ("also . . . Miriam"). The leadership role of Miriam is also diminished in the biblical text. In Psalm 77:20 the name of Miriam is omitted from the list of leaders in Israel: "You led your people like a flock by the hand of Moses and Aaron." Where is Miriam? Her position as a leader of Israel was marginalized by the psalmist. The memory of what Miriam did for the community was forgotten, consigned to an ideology that minimized the contribution of women to their society.

Reading and interpreting the biblical text is not easy. At times, a translator, in order to make sense of a text, applies methods of interpretation that may reflect cultural and theological biases. The NIV diminishes Miriam by omitting her name twice. Furthermore, the addition of the word "also" by the translators of the NIV and the TNIV gives a slant to the text that serves to undervalue the role of Miriam as a leader in Israel. It is impossible to know whether this addition to the text was intentional. However, the resulting translation has a strong theological overtone, one that may reflect an undercurrent of patriarchy. In light of the leadership role Miriam played in the community that came out of Egypt, the translation of Micah 6:4 in the NIV and the TNIV is not acceptable.

1. Anderson and Freedman, *Micah*, 519.

10

Azazel

THE DAY OF ATONEMENT, also known as Yom Kippur, was considered the holiest day in the religious calendar of the people of Israel. The ritual for the Day of Atonement is described in detail in Leviticus 16. In Leviticus 16 God spoke to Moses, giving instructions on how to make atonement for the sins of the priests, of the people, and of the nation. The Day of Atonement was celebrated on the tenth day of the seventh month, and was a day of solemn rest, fasting, and sacrifices. The high priest would enter the Holy of Holies to make atonement for the people and the nation and to make atonement for the tabernacle and the altar. The purpose of this chapter is not to discuss all the events that occurred on the Day of Atonement. Rather, this essay will discuss the selection of the two goats used on the Day of Atonement.

According to the ritual described in Leviticus 16, Aaron must make personal preparations to enter the Holy of Holies. He must bathe in water, put on his holy vestments, and make a sacrifice for himself and for his family. As for the sacrifice for the people, Aaron must take two male goats and place them at the entrance of the tent of meeting. Then, lots would be cast upon the two goats. The English translations differ on how to interpret the selection of the two goats. All translations agree that the first goat was for the Lord. The problem comes with the selection of the second goat.

Below are four translations of Leviticus 16:8–10:

The KJV: "And Aaron shall cast lots upon the two goats; one lot for the LORD, and the other lot for the scapegoat. And Aaron shall bring the goat upon which the LORD'S lot fell, and offer him for a sin offering. But the goat, on which the lot fell to be the scapegoat, shall be presented alive before the LORD, to make an atonement with him, and to let him go for a scapegoat into the wilderness."

The Douay-Rheims: "And casting lots upon them both, one to be offered to the Lord, and the other to be the emissary goat: That whose lot fell to be offered to the Lord, he shall offer for sin: But that whose lot was to be the emissary goat, he shall present alive before the Lord, that he may pour out prayers upon him, and let him go into the wilderness."

The NLT: "He is to cast sacred lots to determine which goat will be reserved as an offering to the LORD and which will carry the sins of the people to the wilderness of Azazel. Aaron will then present as a sin offering the goat chosen by lot for the LORD. The other goat, the scapegoat chosen by lot to be sent away, will be kept alive, standing before the LORD. When it is sent away to Azazel in the wilderness, the people will be purified and made right with the LORD."

The NRSV: "and Aaron shall cast lots on the two goats, one lot for the LORD and the other lot for Azazel. Aaron shall present the goat on which the lot fell for the LORD, and offer it as a sin offering; but the goat on which the lot fell for Azazel shall be presented alive before the LORD to make atonement over it, that it may be sent away into the wilderness to Azazel."

Before the goat was sent away into the wilderness, the high priest would place his hands on the head of the goat, and lay the sins of the people on the goat. After the priest had transferred the sins of the people to the goat, then the goat would be sent out into the wilderness, symbolically carrying away the sins of the community.

There has been a great amount of confusion about the exact meaning of the Hebrew word עֲזָאזֵל ("Azazel"). It is clear from the text that the second goat was not a sacrifice, since the goat was not killed, but sent away into the wilderness carrying away the sins of Israel. The symbolism behind this act was that the goat was removing the sins of the people into the wilderness. However, the exact meaning of the Hebrew word עֲזָאזֵל ("Azazel") is a matter of dispute among scholars. Some believe Azazel was the name of a far-away place, to which the goat was sent in order to remove the sins of the people.

The KJV translates Azazel (עֲזָאזֵל) by dividing the one Hebrew word into two words. The KJV translates the word עֵז as "goat" and the word אזל as "to send." Thus, the translation of the Hebrew word "Azazel" becomes "the scapegoat" or "the goat that goes." The DRA translates Azazel as "the emissary goat." This translation follows the Vulgate (the Latin version of the Bible), which translates the word Azazel as *caper emissarius*. Others believe Azazel was the name of a being. This is the position taken by the NRSV. In the same way the first goat was dedicated to Yahweh (the name of a being), the second was sent to Azazel (the name of a being).

The Bible says the wilderness was the place where demons lived. Leviticus 17:7 reads: "So they shall no more sacrifice their sacrifices to goat demons, after whom they whore" (ESV). If Azazel was the name of a desert demon, then the symbolism behind the ritual was to send evil back to its place of origin. The NLT attempts to make a compromise with the various meanings of the word Azazel. The expression "wilderness of Azazel" could be construed in this translation to be the name of a place. In the translation, "The other goat, the scapegoat chosen by lot," the word Azazel is translated as "scapegoat," while the expression "to Azazel in the wilderness" is clearly a reference to a being.

Thus, it is evident from the translations cited above that the meaning of Azazel is uncertain. Some translations use the term "scapegoat" while others use Azazel as the name of a being. However, since the name Azazel stands in a parallel relationship with Yahweh in verses 9–10, it is clear the name Azazel refers either to a place or to a demon that lived in the wilderness.

11

Understanding Numbers 24:24

THE INTERPRETATION OF NUMBERS 24:24 is not easy because of the problems of translation and the issues raised by the text. Below is a review of how three translations have dealt with Numbers 24:24 and a proposed explanation of the message of the text.

Numbers 24:24 is a section of the Balaam cycle. Balaam was the son of Beor. He was a diviner employed by Balak the son of Zippor, king of Moab, to curse Israel. According to the biblical text, Balaam tried to curse Israel, but God told Balaam to bless Israel. Unable to curse Israel, Balaam told Balak to entice Israel by engaging Israelite men into having sexual relations with the women of Moab. There are seven oracles in the Balaam cycle. Numbers 24:23–24 is Balaam's seventh oracle, an oracle against Asshur and Eber. The three examples below reflect the ways the versions have translated Numbers 24:24:

NRSV: "But ships shall come from Kittim and shall afflict Asshur and Eber; and he also shall perish forever."

DRA: "They shall come in galleys from Italy, they shall overcome the Assyrians, and shall waste the Hebrews, and at the last they themselves also shall perish."

NKJV: "But ships shall come from the coasts of Cyprus, and they shall afflict Asshur and afflict Eber, and so shall Amalek, until he perishes."

According to the text, Kittim refers to a place from which a group of invaders will come in ships to conquer Asshur and Eber. The name Kittim is probably a reference to a city in Cyprus named Kition. Kittim is also used to designate Cyprus (Isa 23:1). The invaders from Kittim have been identified with the Sea Peoples, and more specifically with the Philistines. In the Septuagint of Daniel 11:30 the word Kittim is translated as "Romans," a view adopted by the DRA and the NIrV: "Roman ships will oppose him" (Dan 11:30 NIrV). In 1 Maccabees 1:1, Kittim refers to the Greeks: "After Alexander son of Philip, the Macedonian, who came from the land of Kittim" (1 Mac 1:1). In the literature of Qumran, Kittim becomes a word to describe the eschatological enemies of God.

Asshur has been identified with the Assyrian empire that dominated the ancient Near East from the ninth to the seventh centuries B.C. Some scholars have identified the word "Asshur" with the Asshurim (NIV: Ashurites), a nomadic group who lived in the Negev (Gen 25:3). If Asshur is a reference to the Asshurim, then Eber must be one of their neighbors.

The name Eber appears in the genealogy of Shem (Gen 11:14–17). Some have identified Eber with the inhabitants of Mesopotamia. The Septuagint translates the name Eber as "Hebrews." The DRA follows the Septuagint and translates Kittim as Italy and Eber as Hebrews.

The NKJV adds the word "Amalek" to verse 24. The word "Amalek" does not appear in the Hebrew text. The word comes from verse 20. It seems the translators of the NKJV wanted to emphasize that Amalek was one of the nations that would also be destroyed.

Various interpretations have been proposed to solve the difficulties offered by the text. The most probable interpretation and one that has satisfied a number of commentators is that the words of Balaam are an oracle alluding to the conquest of the Moabites (Num 24:17), the Edomites (Num 24:18), the Amalekites (Num 24:20), and the Philistines (Num 24:24). Thus, Numbers 24:24 says the invaders from Kittim, that is the Philistines, would conquer the Asshurim and the Hebrews (the Israelites), but the Philistines would also be conquered and destroyed. The defeat of the Philistines was accomplished by David after he established his kingdom.

SECTION TWO

The Historical Books

12

The Levite and His Concubine

THE STORY OF THE Levite and his concubine in Judges 19:1–30 is a sad story. It is a story that brings together a man and a woman who lived in the chaotic days preceding the establishment of the monarchy in Israel. It was a time when "there was no king in Israel" and "people did what was right in their own eyes" (Judg 17:6). Phyllis Trible describes the tragic story of the Levite and his concubine as a "text of terror."[1]

The biblical text presents the story of a woman, the concubine of a Levite, who leaves her home to return to the house of her father. The Levite, a man from Ephraim, goes to Bethlehem to bring his concubine back with him to their home. After much reluctance on the woman's part, and at the insistence of her father, the woman agrees to return home with her husband. On the way back they spent the night in Gibeah of Benjamin. While in Gibeah, some men of the city attempted to have a homosexual affair with the Levite. Because of his fear of violence against him, the Levite gives his concubine to the men of the city, who raped her over and over again all that night. The next morning the woman dies; the Levite cut her into twelve pieces and sent the parts of her body to the twelve tribes of Israel. In light of the tragedy that resulted in the woman's death and the dismemberment of her body by the hands of her own husband, a question lingers: why did she leave her home to return to her father's house? Why did she leave the protection of her husband?

According to the KJV, she left her home because she had played the whore against him: "And his concubine played the whore against him, and

---

1. Trible, *Texts of Terror*.

went away from him unto her father's house to Bethlehemjudah" (Judg 19:2). Thus, according to the KJV, the woman committed adultery and for that reason, she left her husband.

The NIV only says that she was unfaithful to him: "But she was unfaithful to him. She left him and went back to her parents' home in Bethlehem, Judah." The view that the woman was unfaithful to her husband and had committed adultery is assumed by the ASV, the DBA, the ESV, the JPS, the NAB, the NASB, the TNIV, the NKJV, the NLT, and the HCSB.

In his commentary on Judges, Matthew Henry writes: "Had her husband turned her out of doors unjustly, her father ought to have pitied her affliction; but, when she treacherously departed from her husband to embrace the bosom of a stranger, her father ought not to have countenanced her sin. Perhaps she would not have violated her duty to her husband if she had not known too well where she should be kindly received."[2]

Matthew Henry also writes: "The Levite went himself to court her return. It was a sign there was no king, no judge, in Israel, else she would have been prosecuted and put to death as an adulteress; but, instead of that, she is addressed in the kindest manner by her injured husband, who takes a long journey on purpose to beseech her to be reconciled, v. 3. If he had put her away, it would have been a crime in him to return to her again, Jer. iii. 1. But, she having gone away, it was a virtue in him to forgive the offence, and, though the party wronged, to make the first motion to her to be friends again."[3] But, what is wrong with this statement? It is hard to believe that in a land where honor killing was very common, a woman who played the whore against her husband, one who had been unfaithful to the marriage relationship, would be allowed to return to her father's house.

When Judah discovered his daughter-in-law Tamar was pregnant, he was indignant. When Judah was told, "Your daughter-in-law Tamar has played the whore; moreover she is pregnant as a result of whoredom," Judah was enraged: "Bring her out, and let her be burned" (Gen 38:24). The same fate should have fallen upon the Levite's concubine, but it did not. Therefore, there must be another explanation.

The word translated "played the whore" and "unfaithful" in Hebrew is zānah. The word has a primary meaning of committing fornication, being a harlot.[4] However, according to Koehler-Baumgartner, the word also can

2. Henry, "Judges," 235.
3. Ibid.
4. BDB, 275.

44

mean "to be angry, hateful" or to "feel repugnant against."[5] Thus, taking the above meaning of the word, the translation of the NRSV makes better sense: "But his concubine became angry with him, and she went away from him to her father's house at Bethlehem in Judah." This is the view also adopted by some ancient translations such as the Septuagint, the Targum, and the Vulgate. None of these ancient translations or Josephus accused the woman of conjugal infidelity. The view that the woman left her husband because of a domestic quarrel is adopted by the RSV, the NRSV, the NEB, the BBE, and the NJB.

It is clear this reading of Judges 19:2 does not presuppose an act of conjugal infidelity by the Levite's concubine. This translation points to the fact the husband and wife had a fight and in anger the woman left her husband and returned to her father's house. The social and cultural backgrounds of the story tend to affirm the correctness of this translation. If the concubine had played the whore and been unfaithful to her husband, her husband would not have gone after his concubine to return her to his home. Since she was a secondary wife, it is quite probable he would have invoked the tradition of honor killing and had her put to death for her unfaithfulness.

The KJV's translation places the blame for the problem on the woman: she was the one who committed adultery and left. The NRSV's translation places the blame on the husband: he did something so outrageous that, in anger, she left the security of her home to find security in the house of her father. In his explanation of what happened between the Levite and his concubine, Josephus wrote: "They quarreled one with another perpetually; and at last the woman was so disgusted at these quarrels, that she left her husband and went [back] to her parents."[6] It is evident that this rereading of Judges 19:2 reflects a better understanding of what happened between the Levite and his concubine. The fact seems to be the husband and wife had a big fight, she probably was afraid for her life, and she tried to find security and protection in the house of her father.

The end of the story seems to demonstrate the basis for her fear. The Levite left his home to "speak to her heart," to convince her to come home. Although the father of the woman was eager for reconciliation, it seems she was reluctant to go with him. His willingness to sacrifice his concubine in order to save his honor may indicate the woman's fear was real. His selfishness demonstrates that in the end, he loved himself more than he loved her.

5. Koehler-Baumgartner, *Lexicon*, 261.

6. Josephus, *Ant.* 5:2.

It becomes imperative that the biblical text be reread in light of this new understanding of the social and cultural conditions of ancient Israel. Today's generation of Bible students need to know this unnamed woman was not a whore nor was she unfaithful to her husband. Only by rereading the text will today's readers discover that all the accusations lodged against this woman were false. May this rereading of the text vindicate her reputation.

Rest in peace.

13

The Sacrifice of Jephthah's Daughter

THE STORY OF JEPHTHAH is well known by readers of the Bible because of his willingness to sacrifice his daughter to celebrate his victory against the enemies of Israel (Judg 10:6—12:7). Jephthah was the commander of the Israelite army in Gilead at the time the Ammonites were oppressing Israel. The leaders of Israel selected Jephthah to fight for them. After the Spirit of the Lord endued Jephthah with power to defeat Israel's enemies, he went to war against the Ammonites, the people who had oppressed Israel for eighteen years (Judg 10:8). Before going to war, Jephthah made a vow to the Lord. In his vow Jephthah promised to make a sacrifice to the Lord in exchange for a victory against his enemies. Jephthah said: "If you will give the Ammonites into my hand, then whoever comes out of the doors of my house to meet me, when I return victorious from the Ammonites, shall be the Lord's, to be offered up by me as a burnt offering" (Judg 11:30–31 NRSV).

When Jephthah returned to his home in Mizpah victorious from his war against the Ammonites, his only daughter came out in celebration to meet him. Jephthah was grieved by the fact that it was his daughter who came out to meet him. In grief, he tore his clothes and said: "Alas, my daughter! You have brought me very low" (Judg 11:35). Jephthah's grief overwhelms his daughter; however, she does not lament her fate. Rather, she asks her father's permission to go to the hills for two months to lament her virginity. After two months she returns, and Jephthah "did to her as he had vowed" (Judg 11:39 TNK).

The NIV and several other translations differ in the way they translate Judges 11:31. The intent of this change is to mitigate the moral dilemma raised by the fact that Jephthah, a man who is celebrated as a "hero of the faith" in Hebrews 11:32, makes a human sacrifice to Yahweh. The NIV reads: "if you give the Ammonites into my hands, whatever comes out of the door of my house to meet me when I return in triumph from the Ammonites will be the Lord's, and I will sacrifice it as a burnt offering" (Judg 11:30–31).

The "whoever" of the NRSV presupposes a person, a human being. The "whatever" of the NIV presupposes an animal. The following translations use "whoever": LXX, BBE, CEB, NAB, NET, NRSV, and the RSV. The following translations use "whatever" or a similar word: ASV, CJB, HCSB, ERV, ESV, GWN, JPS, KJV, NAS, NIV, NKJV, NLT, RWB, TNIV, and the TNK.

The GBV translates "that thing" and the NJB translates "the first thing." The translation of the DB is neutral; it reads: "that which cometh forth." The REB is also neutral: "the first creature that comes out of the door of my house." The GNB is not neutral: "I will burn as an offering the first person that comes out of my house to meet me." So, the question arises: was Jephthah expecting an animal or a person to come out and meet him when he returned home victorious? Did Jephthah make a vow to offer a human sacrifice to God? Adam Clarke in his commentary on Judges writes: "Therefore it must be granted that he never made that rash vow which several suppose he did; nor was he capable, if he had, of executing it in that most shocking manner which some Christian writers ('tell it not in Gath') have contended for."[1]

In order to demonstrate that Jephthah did not make a human sacrifice, Clarke changes the Hebrew וְהַעֲלִיתִהוּ עוֹלָה (weha 'ălîtihû 'ôlāh "I will offer it a burnt-offering") to וְהַעֲלִיתִי הוּא עוֹלָה (weha 'ălîtî hû' 'ôlāh "I will offer Him [i.e., the Lord] a burnt-offering").[2] Clarke's emendation of the text changes the meaning of the passage. The revised text reads as follows: "Whatsoever comes out of the doors of my house to meet me, shall be the Lord's; and I will offer Him a burnt-offering." Thus, the "whatever" translation removes the stigma of human sacrifice from the text. The "whatever" translation allows for an animal sacrifice to be made to God. The "whatever" translation also clears Jephthah from a barbarous act. Jephthah's words, however, clearly indicate he intended to sacrifice a human being, not an animal, for only a person living in his household could be expected to come out and meet him. If Jephthah had intended to offer an animal sacrifice, he probably would have promised to offer the best of his flock.

It was common in the ancient Near East to celebrate victories with music. Israel, like all its neighbors, also celebrated victories in battle with

---

1. Clarke, "Judges," 641.
2. Ibid., 640.

music and dancing. Music and dancing served as a natural expression of joy. In Israel, dancing was part of the victory celebration, as can be seen in the case of Jephthah's daughter. One example of the use of music and dancing in times of celebration is Miriam leading Israelite women in celebration at the time the waters of the Red Sea (Sea of Reeds) parted and allowed the people of Israel to cross the sea safely. After the Egyptians drowned in the sea, Miriam "took a tambourine in her hand; and all the women went out after her with tambourines and dancing" (Exod 15:20). Another example of music and dancing to celebrate victory in battle is found in 1 Samuel 18:6. When Saul and David returned home after their victory against the Philistines, "the women came out . . . with singing and dancing, to meet King Saul, with tambourines, with songs of joy, and with musical instruments" (1 Sam 18:6). The "Song of Deborah" (Judg 5:1–31) could also be considered a song of celebration, even though the text does not say the women came out to meet Deborah and Barak with music and dancing after their victory against Sisera and the army of the Canaanites.

Thus, when Jephthah returned home victorious from his struggle with the Ammonites, his daughter came out to meet him, dancing to the sound of tambourines (Judg 11:34). This was the custom in Israel: when the people were victorious against their enemy, the victory was celebrated with music and dancing. But Jephthah probably expected a servant to come out and welcome him, not his only daughter. So, Jephthah fulfilled his vow to the Lord. When his daughter returned home after two months in the mountains, Jephthah "did to her as he had vowed" (Judg 11:39). But, an important question must be asked in the fulfilling of Jephthah's vow. If Jephthah did to his daughter what he had vowed to do, then, what did Jephthah do? And there is a lot of debate about the answer to this question and to what happened to Jephthah's daughter. What happened to Jephthah's daughter will be discussed in the next chapter.

14

The Fate of Jephthah's Daughter

IN THE PREVIOUS CHAPTER I wrote about the problem various versions of the Bible have in translating Judges 11:31. The correct translation of verse 31 is crucial to the proper understanding of the fate of Jephthath's daughter. This is how the RSV translates Judges 11:30–31: "And Jephthah made a vow to the Lord, and said, 'If thou wilt give the Ammonites into my hand, then whoever comes forth from the doors of my house to meet me, when I return victorious from the Ammonites, shall be the Lord's, and I will offer him up for a burnt offering.'"

This is how the NIV translates Judges 11:30–31: "And Jephthah made a vow to the Lord: 'If you give the Ammonites into my hands, whatever comes out of the door of my house to meet me when I return in triumph from the Ammonites will be the Lord's, and I will sacrifice it as a burnt offering.'" The "whoever" of the RSV presupposes that Jephthah expected a human being to meet him. The "whatever" of the NIV presupposes that either an animal or a person would come out of the house. However, the "him" of the RSV and the "it" of the NIV make clear the translators of the NIV had an animal in mind.

On his return, Jephthah's daughter came to meet him. In his distress, Jephthah bemoaned the fact he would have to sacrifice her. His daughter asked permission to go away for two months, and upon her return, Jephthah "did with her according to his vow which he had made" (Judg 11:39). The question to be asked is: if Jephthah did with his daughter what he vowed to do, then what did Jephthah do with his daughter? The simple answer is: he sacrificed her as a burnt offering to God. This is the simple meaning of the text. The promise Jephthah made to God was that whoever came from his house to meet him, he would offer him up to the Lord as a burnt offering. Or, as the GNB puts it: "I will burn as an offering the first person that comes out of my house to meet me when I come back from victory. I will offer that person to you as a sacrifice" (Judg 11:31). The word עֹלָה (*ʿolāh*) is often translated as a "holocaust" or "burnt offering." When the offerer made an *ʿolāh* sacrifice, the sacrifice was completely burned.

Some scholars disagree with the view that Jephthah's daughter was sacrificed to God. They believe verse 39 is not clear and does not tell what Jephthah did with his daughter. Thus, these writers believe Jephthah did not sacrifice his daughter as a burnt offering to God. In his commentary on Judges, Adam Clarke writes: "Therefore it must be granted that he never made that rash vow which several suppose he did; nor was he capable, if he had, of executing it in that most shocking manner which some Christian writers ('tell it not in Gath') have contended for."[1]

Clarke emended the text to read that Jephthah will offer a sacrifice to the Lord to celebrate his victory against the enemies of Israel. The reason Clarke did not believe Jephthah sacrificed his daughter to the Lord was because Jephthah was a pious man who was endowed with the Spirit of God (Judg 11:29). Since the Spirit of God was upon Jephthah, Clarke says, "that Spirit could not permit him to imbrue his hands in the blood of his own child; and especially under the pretense of offering a pleasing sacrifice to that God who is the Father of mankind, and the Fountain of love, mercy, and compassion."[2]

His conclusion, then, is that Jephthah did not sacrifice his daughter to God, but consecrated her to serve the Lord in a state of perpetual virginity. His view is based on the words "she had never known a man" (v. 39). According to Clarke, persons who were dedicated or consecrated to God would live in a state of celibacy until death. C. F. Keil, in his commentary on Judges takes the same approach. Keil writes:

> And so, again, the still further clause in the account of the fulfil-
> ment of the vow, "and she knew no man," is not in harmony with
> the assumption of a sacrificial death. This clause would add noth-
> ing to the description in that case, since it was already known that
> she was a virgin. The words only gain their proper sense if we con-
> nect them with the previous clause, he "did with her according to
> the vow which he had vowed," and understand them as describing
> what the daughter did in fulfillment of the vow. The father fulfilled

1. Clarke, "Judges," 641.
2. Ibid.

his vow upon her, and she knew no man; i.e., he fulfilled the vow
through the fact that she knew no man, but dedicated her life to
the Lord, as a spiritual burnt-offering, in a lifelong chastity.[3]

Clarke's and Keil's views are based on the interpretation of Rabbi David Kimchi (1160–1235), a Middle Age Jewish scholar, who believed Jephthah had
not sacrificed his daughter to God. Rather, Kimchi believed Jephthah dedicated his daughter to serve in one of the sanctuaries of the Lord as a virgin for
the rest of her life. A closer look at the text reveals the better interpretation of
what happened in this situation, and let it be told in Gath, was that Jephthah
actually sacrificed his daughter as an offering for the Lord.

Jephthah was a man without honor. He was the son of a prostitute (Judg
11:1) and was expelled from his father's house because he was an "illegitimate
son." He was a man rejected by the leaders of Gilead because of his illegitimate birth and he became the leader of a group of men of low character who
went out raiding with him. Jephthah's only honor was the honor of his word,
but even this some scholars are trying to take away from him. Jephthah said
to his daughter: "Alas, my daughter! you have brought me very low, and you
have become the cause of great trouble to me; for I have opened my mouth to
the Lord, and I cannot take back my vow" (Judg 11:35).

In the society where Jephthah lived, a vow was sacred to God: "When
you make a vow to the Lord your God, you shall not be slack to pay it; for
the Lord your God will surely require it of you, and it would be sin in you"
(Deut 23:21 RSV). The sacredness of a vow is also reflected in Psalm 15. The
psalmist asked: "O Lord, who shall sojourn in thy tent? Who shall dwell on
thy holy hill?" (Ps 15:1). And the answer was: he "who swears to his own
hurt and does not change" (v. 4).

Jephthah's daughter recognized her father had made a vow that could
not be retracted. She said: "My father, if you have opened your mouth to the
Lord, do to me according to what has gone forth from your mouth" (Judg
11:36 RSV). A Christian who lives by the teaching of Christ may recoil at the
fact that a follower of the Lord actually sacrificed his daughter to God, but
he did and in the end, he was praised as a hero of the faith in Hebrews 11:32.

The Lord delivered Israel not because Jephthah made a vow, but because the Lord desired to save his people. Jephthah's fulfillment of his vow
is due to his ignorance and lack of knowledge about the true nature of the
God of Israel. Ironically, it is precisely in this act of being faithful to the
promise he made to God that we can see Jephthah's dedication to God.

3. Keil, *Joshua, Judges, Ruth*, 393.

Although human sacrifice does not appear in Israel until the days of Ahaz and Manasseh, Solomon dedicated temples to Chemosh and Molech (1 Kgs 11:7), gods to whom human sacrifices were made. Human sacrifice was known in pre-monarchic Israel, but generally, it was dedicated to pagan gods. There is no doubt some people in Israel believed human sacrifice was a great demonstration of faith and dedication to God. When the people asked the prophet Micah, "Shall I give my firstborn for my transgression, the fruit of my body for the sin of my soul?" (Mic 6:7), their question assumes some people believed human sacrifice, under certain conditions, was acceptable to God.

So, the only obvious interpretation of the words of the writer of the book of Judges, that Jephthah "did with her according to his vow which he had made" (Judg 11:39), is Jephthah offered his daughter as a human sacrifice to God, and in his mind and in the minds of some people in Israel, that kind of sacrifice was the best offering one could offer to God.

In the next chapter I will conclude my study of the sacrifice of Jephthah's daughter with a study of the words "she had never known a man" (Judg 11:39).

15

The Virginity of Jephthah's Daughter

THIS FINAL ESSAY ON Jephthah's daughter will deal with the issue of her virginity. There is no question she was a virgin to the day of her death. On this issue, all scholars agree. The issue of her virginity is directly related to the manner in which she died. The translation of Judges 11:39 affects the way her death is interpreted. What follows is the way the RSV and the NIV translate Judges 11:39: "And at the end of two months, she returned to her father, who did with her according to his vow which he had made. She had never known a man" (Judg 11:39 RSV). "After the two months, she returned to her father, and he did to her as he had vowed. And she was a virgin" (Judg 11:39 NIV). To the average reader, the two translations are identical. The only difference in the two translations is found in the words the translators used to describe her sexual condition: "she had never known a man" and "she was a virgin." However, for the interpreter of the text, the way the text is translated affects the way the text is interpreted. C. J. Goslinga explains how the translation of Judges 11:39 affects the interpretation of the text. Goslinga writes:

> It is hard to translate these words without opting for a particular interpretation of the text. The most obvious translation would be "and she had never known a man" (cf. RSV), but the preceding clause would then have to mean that Jephthah sacrificed his daughter. A more neutral but equally permissible translation would be "she had no relations with a man," or "she was a virgin." The meaning would be that she remained celibate her entire life and died a virgin. Such translation is therefore preferable. It does not contradict the thought that she was killed, but it also leaves open the possibility that she lived on as a virgin.[1]

1. Goslinga, *Joshua, Judges, Ruth*, 391, n. 182.

Goslinga is very clear: the translation of the RSV, "she had never known a man," which he calls "the most obvious translation," implies that Jephthah sacrificed his daughter. The translation of the NIV, "she was a virgin," means she was not sacrificed, but rather, she remained celibate for the rest of her life. The ambiguity of the text forces the interpreter to ask questions. Is the text saying after she returned from her retreat she knew no man after, that is, she never had sex until she died? Or is the text saying she was sacrificed as a virgin? C. F. Keil takes the former view. In his commentary of Judges, he writes: "To mourn one's virginity does not mean to mourn because one has to die a virgin, but because one has to live and remain a virgin."[2] Keil then explains the words "and she knew no man":

> The clause in the account of the fulfilment of the vow, "and she knew no man," is not in harmony with the assumption of a sacrificial death. This clause would add nothing to the description in that case, since it was already known that she was a virgin. The words only gain their proper sense if we connect them with the previous clause, he "did with her according to the vow which he had vowed," and understand them as describing what the daughter did in fulfilment of the vow. The father fulfilled his vow upon her, and she knew no man; i.e., he fulfilled the vow through the fact that she knew no man, but dedicated her life to the Lord, as a spiritual burnt-offering, in a lifelong chastity.[3]

Even Goslinga struggled in deciding what happened to Jephthah's daughter. He wavered between the fact the text requires her death and the view it was hard to understand "how a man like Jephthah could have taken a vow that obligated him to offer a human sacrifice." He then concluded:

> In my view the words of verse 39, which conceal more than they reveal, do not absolutely rule out the possibility of permanent separation. Jephthah's daughter could indeed have been put to death, but there could also have been a mournful ceremony in which she was sent off into the desert to wither and die. The words "and she was a virgin" would then make clear what Jephthah's decision did to her, and the custom reported in verse 40 could have been a means to lighten her unbearable fate a little by allowing her to have company for four days a year.[4]

2. Keil, *Joshua, Judges, Ruth*, 393.
3. Ibid.
4. Goslinga, 395.

I sympathize with people who are uneasy with the outcome of this passage. It is hard to believe a man endowed with the Spirit of God would offer human sacrifice to the God of Israel, but he did. Jephthah's action should not be interpreted in light of the teachings of Jesus Christ. After all, Jephthah was a B.C. man.

The near sacrifice of Isaac in Genesis 22 reveals the reality of human sacrifice was a possibility in the world of ancient Israel. However, if Genesis 22 is a polemic against human sacrifice, then the greatest lesson to be learned from the near sacrifice of Isaac is that human sacrifice was not to be a part of the religion of the God of Abraham.

Jephthah's daughter, unfortunately, was sacrificed as a burnt offering. The dedication of Samuel to God in 1 Samuel 1:11–28 is not a good precedent for the view that the sacrifice of Jephthah's daughter was just a "spiritual sacrifice." The sacrifice of Jephthah's daughter is not the focus of Jephthah's narrative; the real focus of the story is the irrevocability of a vow. As Boling writes: "The fact of human sacrifice in Jephthah's story is secondary to the theme of the irrevocability of the vow." Although Boling believed the "whatever" of verse 31 could be a reference to a domesticated animal, his view that the writer of the book of Judges is sympathetic with Jephthah and his conclusion that the focus of the story is the writer's portrayal "of Jephthah's integrity in fulfilling his vow" is correct.[5]

Students of the Bible will continue to discuss the sacrifice of Jephthah's daughter and whether Jephthah actually offered his daughter as a burnt offering to God. Those who reject the view that she was not sacrificed, do so without much textual support. The issue of how one views the fate of Jephthah's daughter also affects the manner in which the text is translated. Bible translators cannot allow personal preferences to influence the way a text is translated. However, this is easier said than done. Each translation is an interpretation of the text. The responsibility of the translator is to translate the text as the text appears in the manuscripts without conveying a meaning that is not present in the text. For instance, to translate 2 Samuel 21:19, that Elhanan killed the brother of Goliath, as the TNIV does, is wrong because those words are not in the text. The words of Judges 11:31 and 11:39 are more difficult to translate because of the ambiguity already present in the text. The translator here must be faithful to the text and leave it to the interpreter to decide what the text means.

5. Boling, Judges, 210.

16

Who Went Back to the City?

THE BOOK OF RUTH presents a beautiful story of unselfish love. The book narrates the story of two widows who lost their husbands and became destitute. Ruth and Naomi became widows in the land of Moab and then returned to Bethlehem, the birthplace of Naomi. The book is also a love story. It is the story of Ruth the Moabite widow who decided to leave her country and follow her mother-in-law Naomi to Bethlehem. Upon their return, Ruth met a rich man whose name was Boaz, a prominent man who was also a landowner in Bethlehem. The love affair between Ruth and Boaz began when Ruth came to glean in the field that belonged to Boaz. When Boaz came to inspect his workers during the harvest of barley, he saw Ruth and took an interest in her.

Boaz had heard what Ruth had done for her mother-in-law and how she had decided to follow Naomi and come to Bethlehem after the death of her husband. Boaz was so impressed by Ruth's selflessness that he decided to help her. At the end of the day, when she finished gathering what she had threshed, she returned to Naomi and gave to her mother-in-law some of the food that was left over from the food she received from Boaz. Ruth worked in Boaz's field until the end of the barley and the wheat harvests. At the end of the harvest, Naomi realized Ruth should marry Boaz, since he was a close relative and the family's *goel*, a kinsman redeemer. So, Naomi told Ruth to dress up, put some perfume, go to the threshing floor, and spend the night there.

That night, after Boaz finished eating, he came to the threshing floor and went to sleep. Ruth slept by his side. In the middle of the night, Boaz awoke and realized Ruth was by his side. He told her to stay there with him until morning. In the morning, Boaz gave Ruth six measures of barley and then someone went back to the city. But, who went back to the city? It depends on what translation one reads. The Revised Standard Version reads: "And [Boaz] said, 'Bring the mantle you are wearing and hold it out.' So she held it, and he measured out six measures of barley, and laid it upon her; *then she went into the city*" (Ruth 3:15 RSV, emphasis mine).

The New Revised Standard Version reads: "Then [Boaz] said, 'Bring the cloak you are wearing and hold it out.' So she held it, and he measured out six measures of barley, and put it on her back; *then he went into the city*" (Ruth 3:15 NRSV, emphasis mine).

The versions disagree on who went back to the city. The following versions agree with the Revised Standard Version and say Ruth went back to the city: The BBE, DRA, ESV, GBV, HCSB, JPS, TNK, KJV, NASB, NJB, NKJV, and the RWB. The following versions agree with the New Revised Standard Version and say Boaz went back to the city: ASV, CJB, DBY, ERV, GWN, NET, NAB, NASB, NIV, NLT, TNIV, and the YLT.

Why such a discrepancy? Why do the versions differ in their translation of the text? The reason for this difference is because several Hebrew manuscripts have the masculine form of the verb, "he went back to the city," while many other manuscripts have the feminine form of the verb, "she went back the city." In addition, the feminine reading is supported by the Syriac version and by the Vulgate. One reason to adopt the feminine form of the verb and say it was Ruth who returned back to the city is that the context seems to require it. This is seen in what Ruth did after she returned to the city. Here is how verse 15 reads and how verse 16 begins: "And [Boaz] said, 'Bring the mantle you are wearing and hold it out.' So she held it, and he measured out six measures of barley, and laid it upon her; then she went into the city. And when she came to her mother-in-law . . ." (Ruth 3:15–16 RSV). Thus, the context seems to indicate it was Ruth who returned back to the city.

17

Was Ruth Barren?

WAS RUTH BARREN? THE reason for this question comes from a dubious interpretation of what the KJV says about Ruth after she married Boaz. The KJV reads: "So Boaz took Ruth, and she was his wife: and when he went in unto her, the LORD gave her conception, and she bare a son" (Ruth 4:13). One interpretation of this text, based on the reading of the KJV, says that, after Boaz purchased the land that belonged to Naomi and her dead husband, and after Boaz acquired Ruth and the right to raise the name of Ruth's dead husband by exercising the right of kinsman-redeemer, Ruth and Boaz had a son because the Lord "gave her conception." According to this interpretation, Ruth was barren and tried to have a child, but unsuccessfully. But, after she married Boaz, the Lord opened her womb and she conceived and gave birth to a son whom the women of Bethlehem named Obed (Ruth 4:17).

The statement that Ruth was barren is not found in the Old Testament. The Old Testament lists five women who were barren. The five barren women were Sarah (Gen 11:30), Rebekah (Gen 25:21), Rachel (Gen 29:30), Hannah (1 Sam 1:2), and Manoah's wife (Samson's mother, cf. Judg 13:2). The New Testament says Elizabeth, the mother of John the Baptist, was also barren (Luke 1:7). But nowhere does the text say Ruth was barren.

The Hebrew word for "barren" is עֲקָרָה, 'ăqārāh. The word appears eleven times in the Old Testament; however, the word is never used in the book of Ruth. Since the Bible does not say Ruth was barren, is there a clue in the book that may indicate Ruth was barren?

There are two possible clues in the book that may indicate Ruth was barren and unable to have children. The first clue is found in Ruth 1:2–4. The text says Elimelech and his wife Naomi had two sons, Mahlon and

Chilion. Because of a famine in Bethlehem, in the land of Judah, Elimelech and his family moved to the country of Moab and lived there many years. In Moab, Mahlon and Chilion "took Moabite wives; the name of the one was Orpah and the name of the other Ruth. They lived there about ten years" (Ruth 1:4). After the death of Mahlon and Chilion, Naomi returned to Bethlehem with Ruth, while Orpah decided to remain in Moab. Thus, since Mahlon and Ruth were married ten years, and Ruth had no children, it is possible Ruth did not have a child because she was barren.

The second clue is found in Ruth 4:13, where it says that after Ruth married Boaz, "the LORD gave her conception, and she bore a son." The idea here is that since the Lord blessed Ruth with conception, then, it is possible Ruth was barren and unable to conceive before the Lord blessed her. However, there are several clues within the book of Ruth that indicate Ruth was not barren. Although these clues may not be conclusive, I believe they point to the fact Ruth was not barren. Below are several reasons for affirming Ruth was not barren.

First, the names of Naomi's two sons may indicate the root of the problem. The name Mahlon comes from a Hebrew word *hlh*, which means "to be weak," or "sick." It is possible Mahlon's name indicates he was a sickly child. The name Chilion comes from a Hebrew word that means "failing," or "consumption." Consumption is a wasting disease such as tuberculosis. Thus, it is possible that Naomi's children were sick from infancy and their disease did not allow them to father children.

Second, both Ruth and Orpah were married to Naomi's sons and the biblical text seems to indicate that both Ruth and Orpah did not have children when their husbands died. So, if Orpah was childless when she became a widow, it is possible the reason that caused Ruth to be a childless widow was the same reason that also caused Orpah to become a childless widow. That reason was their husbands who probably were sterile because of their illness.

Naomi mentioned to Ruth and Orpah the possibility of levirate marriage, where the two widows could have children through another son by Naomi. But Naomi said she was not pregnant and she was too old to remarry and give birth to children. Naomi's words clearly indicate she believed that Ruth and Orpah could become pregnant if they remarried.

Third, when Ruth married Boaz, it is quite possible that Boaz was an old man. When Boaz called Ruth "my daughter" (Ruth 2:8), this may indicate that there was an age differential between Boaz and Ruth. The age issue appears again in Ruth 3:10. Boaz said to Ruth: "May you be blessed by the

LORD, my daughter; you have made this last kindness greater than the first, in that you have not gone after young men, whether poor or rich."

Thus, when Boaz married Ruth, Boaz was older than Ruth. After the marriage, Ruth had no problem becoming pregnant: "So Boaz married Ruth and had sexual relations with her. The LORD enabled her to conceive and she gave birth to a son" (Ruth 4:13 NET). The fact the Lord enabled Ruth to conceive was not because she was barren, rather because the child was seen as a gift from God.

The idea that the child was God's gift is seen in Ruth 4:12. After the wedding, the women of Bethlehem blessed Boaz with the following words: "May your house become like the house of Perez, the son Tamar bore to Judah, because of the offspring the LORD will give you by this young woman" (HCSB). The reference to "your house" and "the offspring the LORD will give you" may indicate Boaz was a childless man, and that God blessed him by allowing his new wife to give birth to a son. Thus, it is my firm conviction that Ruth was not barren.

18

King Saul: Little in His Own Eyes

SAUL WAS THE FIRST king of Israel. He came to the throne at a time when the nation faced great challenges. In a nation where people were fiercely independent, Saul was able to gain the support of the people and bring the tribes together to confront the threat posed by the Philistines. With the ambivalent support of the prophet Samuel, Saul was placed on the throne because the prophet believed he offered the best hope to unite Israel and rescue the nation from the Philistine menace.

The relationship between Samuel and Saul was rocky almost from the beginning. Samuel represented the old order; Saul represented the new reality in Israel. Many people in Israel were against the centralization of the government. Samuel's attitude toward Saul reflects the sentiment of the people who were against the idea that a human king should rule over the people of God. The rise of the monarchy brought many changes to Israelite society and many people were unhappy with these changes.

The conflict between Samuel and Saul arose because Saul refused to obey the words of the prophet. Saul disobeyed the words of Samuel twice. The first time was when he decided to act as a priest and offer sacrifices in order to keep the people together before a battle against the Philistines (1 Sam 13:8–14). The second time was when Saul spared the life of Agag, king of the Amalekites (1 Sam 15:1–11). Saul's reason for sparing the life of the Amalekite king was that he was trying to please his soldiers, who were beginning to doubt his abilities as king.

Because of Saul's disobedience, Samuel withdrew his support from Saul. The lack of prophetical approval was devastating to Saul. Together with the stress posed by the rise of David, that sense of rejection by Samuel practically destroyed Saul as a leader of Israel. Saul's problem was the same problem faced by people everywhere. People need to find affirmation in their own heart that other people support and affirm them. This sense of affirmation creates personal growth and helps develop strong personalities. On the other hand, when people have the perception, real or imaginary, that they are rejected by others, they develop a sense of inferiority which can be compounded by low self-esteem. The feeling of inferiority that affects so many people in our society comes from different sources. Saul's problem came because of his faulty relationship with Samuel. Saul found himself in a situation where his abilities as a king and attitude toward the responsibility of his office, and his obedience to God's command were denigrated and criticized by Samuel.

Saul had worked hard to be worthy of his office and to please the people around him. He made an attempt at justifying his actions by providing his own rationale for the reasons he failed to abide by the words of Samuel, but he failed. Saul's need for social approval acted as a powerful motivator for his actions. As a king, Saul believed he needed the approval of the people and especially, the approval of Samuel. People with low self-esteem often need the approval of other people in order to give them the required social boost they so desperately seek.

Saul's problem was he forgot who he was. Samuel said to him: "Though you are little in your own eyes, are you not the head of the tribes of Israel? The LORD anointed you king over Israel" (1 Sam 15:17). Saul believed he was a nobody, that nobody cared for him, and yet, he was the king of Israel and the one chosen by God to govern the people. His feelings of inferiority destroyed his kingship.

Many Christians are just like Saul. They believe they are nobodies, that they are not loved and appreciated by people around them. Many Christians do everything to get the approval of others when they already have the approval of God. Christians who have low self-esteem and who suffer from an inferiority complex must know who they are: they are children of God, children of the Great King. As children of the Great King they are also heirs of the promises of God. Christians must remember that in Christ they are very important people. The apostle Paul said Christians are chosen in Christ. In Christ they are adopted as God's children and in Christ they have obtained an eternal inheritance (Eph 1:4–6). The truth is: God's people have no reason to be little in their own eyes because they are the "apple of his eye" (Deut 32:10).

19

How Old Was Saul?

THE BOOKS OF THE Bible have come to us through the work of scribes who carefully preserved the received text. Over a period of hundreds of years, the biblical manuscripts were copied and recopied by hand in order to preserve the traditional reading of what was considered sacred text. No original manuscript of any of the biblical books has survived. A group of scribes called the Masoretes took great care to make copies of the biblical books as accurately as possible. However, in the process of copying from their sources, the scribes made some errors that are present in the manuscripts used today to translate the Bible.

When copying errors are found in the text, scholars make an attempt to restore the text in order to discover the probable word or words used in the original manuscript. At times, however, in attempting to correct the text, scholars have proposed solutions that may contradict one another. One classic example is the textual problem found in 1 Samuel 13:1. The Hebrew text of 1 Samuel 13:1 reads: "Saul was one year old when he began to reign and he reigned over Israel two years." It is clear that as written, the text is not right, for Saul had grown children when he became king of Israel. It is evident that the numbers are missing in the text. Scholars have made different attempts at restoring the text, but their efforts have created more confusion. Below are some attempts made by translators to restore the text.

The NIV translates 1 Samuel 13:1 as follows: "Saul was thirty years old when he became king, and he reigned over Israel forty-two years." The NASB translates as follows: "Saul was forty years old when he began to reign, and he reigned thirty-two years over Israel. The NEB translates as follows: "Saul was fifty years old when he became king, and he reigned over Israel for twenty-two years." *The Modern Reader's Bible*, a translation done by Richard G. Moulton,[1] translates as follows: "Saul was thirty years old when he began to reign and he reigned two years over Israel." The ASV translates as follows: "Saul was forty years old when he began to reign; and when he had reigned two years over Israel. . . ." The KJV translates as follows: "Saul reigned one year; and when he had reigned two years over Israel. . . ." In the New Testament, Acts 13:21 says Saul reigned forty-years over Israel. A good explanation for the length of Saul's reign is found in John Tullock's book, *The Old Testament Story*. Tullock writes:

> The length of Saul's reign is uncertain since a number is missing in the Hebrew text, which simply says, "he reigned . . . and two years" (13:1). Most scholars would say he ruled about twenty-two years. If one takes the biblical evidence, twelve years might be more logical. The ark was captured by the Philistines some time before Saul began to reign. According to 1 Samuel 7:2, it was kept in Kiriath-jearim "some twenty years." It was taken to Jerusalem in the early part of David's reign (2 Sam. 6:1–15), but David reigned for over seven years at Hebron before Jerusalem was captured (2 Sam. 5:5). If this "twenty years" is to be taken literally or even as meaning around twenty years, it would seem to limit Saul's reign to no more than twelve years.[2]

The different readings for the length of Saul's reign in the translations cited above are only possibilities. Thus, if a translation says that Saul was thirty, or forty, or fifty years old when he began to reign and then says that he reigned forty-two, thirty-two, twenty-two, or two years over Israel, that translation is not teaching biblical truth but educated possibilities. The fact is, that since the numbers are contradictory, then one or all of the translations may not be presenting the right information.

This contradiction is the biggest problem in trying to guess the numbers missing in 1 Samuel 13:1. Since most students of the Bible use only one translation and never compare one translation against another, they believe the translation they use says what really happened, when in reality the translation may not reflect historical reality.

For instance, take the translation proposed by the KJV: "Saul reigned one year; and when he had reigned two years over Israel." Readers may believe what follows in 13:2 happened two years after Saul became king.

---

1. Moulton, *The Modern Reader's Bible*.
2. Tullock, *Old Testament Story*, 123.

Other translations, such as the NIV and several others, try to harmonize the book of Acts with the text in Samuel by saying Saul was king for forty-two years, when the length of his reign probably was much shorter.

Thus, 1 Samuel 13:1 must be reread in such a way that it preserves the dignity of the text and the historical realities related to Saul's reign. Lately, several translations are leaving the numbers in the text blank. For instance, the NRSV and other translations translate 1 Samuel 13:1 as follows: "Saul was . . . years old when he began to reign; and he reigned . . . and two years over Israel." This translation is not elegant and is not what most people want to read, but it is better to leave the numbers blank than to convey false information to the reader, even when that information is based on an educated guess.

20

David and Melchizedek

THE STATEMENT IN THE book of Hebrews that Jesus is "a priest after the order of Melchizedek" (Heb 5:6) has baffled many Christians and has produced several interesting interpretations. The purpose of this chapter is to study how David continued the priesthood tradition of Melchizedek and to understand the meaning of the statement in Hebrews that Jesus is a priest after the order of Melchizedek.

Five times in the New Testament, Jesus is called, directly or indirectly, "a priest after the order of Melchizedek" (Heb 5:6, 10; 6:20; 7:11, 17). The text in Hebrews 5:5–10 presents two examples of the designation of Jesus as a high priest:

> So also Christ did not exalt himself to be made a high priest, but was appointed by him who said to him, "You are my Son, today I have begotten you"; as he says also in another place, "You are a priest forever, after the order of Melchizedek." In the days of his flesh, Jesus offered up prayers and supplications, with loud cries and tears, to him who was able to save him from death, and he was heard because of his reverence. Although he was a son, he learned obedience through what he suffered. And being made perfect, he became the source of eternal salvation to all who obey him, being designated by God a high priest after the order of Melchizedek (Heb 5:5–10 ESV).

The proper understanding of Jesus as a priest after the order of Melchizedek must begin with Genesis 14:18, where Melchizedek is introduced for the first time: "And Melchizedek king of Salem brought out bread and wine; he was priest of God Most High." Melchizedek met Abraham when the patriarch returned from the pursuit of Chedorlaomer and the other Mesopotamian kings who had taken Lot as a prisoner of war. In the text, Melchizedek is introduced as the priest of God Most High ("El Elyon") and as the king of Salem. Salem is an ancient name for Jerusalem: "His abode has been established in Salem, his dwelling place in Zion" (Ps 76:2). The identification of Melchizedek has been highly debated in the history of the church. Jewish tradition has identified Melchizedek with Shem, the son of Noah who, according to the chronology in Genesis, survived the flood and lived at a time when Abraham was alive and was his contemporary for a hundred years.

Christian tradition has proposed different interpretations to identify who Melchizedek was. Origen said that Melchizedek was an angel. Others have proposed that he was the Holy Spirit in human form.[1] Many Christians, ancient and contemporary, have said that this is a classic example of a Christophany in the Old Testament; that is, Melchizedek was Jesus Christ himself, who appeared to Abraham in human form.

The concept of Christophany should be rejected because it contradicts the statement in the book of Hebrews that Jesus was designated a priest after the order of Melchizedek. If Melchizedek was Christ then how could Christ become a priest in the likeness of Melchizedek? Another view is that Melchizedek was a type of Christ. The typological interpretation suggests that the priesthood of Melchizedek was a type of Christ's priesthood. As Melchizedek was a priest of the Most High God, so was Jesus. As Melchizedek was a king, so was Jesus. Both Melchizedek and Jesus were royal priests. In the persons of Melchizedek and Jesus the offices of priest and king were combined.[2]

The text in Genesis indicates that Melchizedek was a Canaanite king who reigned in Jerusalem before the city was conquered by David and became the capital of the united monarchy (2 Sam 5:6–10). As king of Jerusalem, Melchizedek combined the offices of priest and king into his official duties. The combination of priesthood and kingship into the office of the king was not uncommon in the ancient Near East. For instance, Ethbaal king of the Sidonians and the father of Jezebel, was also the priest of Astarte (1 Kgs 16:31). So, when David conquered Jerusalem and made the city the capital of his empire, he called the stronghold of Zion "The City of David" (2 Sam 5:9). David incorporated the Jebusites, the indigenous population of Jerusalem, into his state and became their king. Since the king of Jerusalem was also a priest, David became a priest, continuing the tradition

1. Allen, *Hebrews*, 437.
2. Pink, *Gleanings in Genesis*, 159–60.

established by Melchizedek, who was both priest and king. This is what the psalmist is trying to communicate. The words of Psalm 110:4 are addressed to the king: "The Lord has sworn and will not change his mind, 'You are a priest for ever after the order of Melchizedek.'"

The priesthood of Melchizedek became a model for David and his descendants. The descendants of David will be king and they will be priests; this is clearly expressed in 2 Samuel 8:18: "and David's sons were priests." The priesthood of Melchizedek is used by the author of the book of Hebrews to prove the claim that Jesus Christ was a high priest. In Israel, the high priest had to be a Levite and a descendant of Aaron. Since Jesus was from the tribe of Judah and a descendant of David, it was impossible for the writer of Hebrews to say that Jesus was a high priest. But, this is precisely what the author of Hebrews is emphasizing in his writing. As a high priest, Jesus presented a sacrifice for sins. Jesus Christ was the "great high priest who has passed through the heavens" (Heb 4:14). Jesus Christ was the high priest who opened the way for people to approach the throne of grace (the Mercy Seat) with confidence so that they "may receive mercy and find grace to help in time of need" (Heb 4:15–16).

The writer of the book of Hebrews then is saying that Jesus became a high priest, not because he was a descendant of Aaron. Jesus became a high priest after the order of Melchizedek because he was a descendant of David and a legitimate successor of the legacy left by David when he became king of Jerusalem. By saying that Jesus became a priest after the order of Melchizedek, the author of Hebrews is emphasizing that Jesus had "become a priest, not according to a legal requirement concerning bodily descent" (Heb 7:16–17), but because of the promise made to David that he and his descendants would become priests forever after the order of Melchizedek (Ps 110:4). The erroneous view that Genesis 14:18 is a Christophany or that Melchizedek was an angel or even the Holy Spirit makes it difficult for the reader to understand the meaning of the statement that Jesus Christ is a high priest "after the order of Melchizedek."

21

David's Sons Were Priests

AFTER DAVID CONQUERED JERUSALEM and made the city the capital of his government, he incorporated the original inhabitants of Jerusalem into the population of Israel and became their king. David became a priest of the people who lived in Jerusalem, not because he was a Levite, but because he continued the tradition established by Melchizedek. Melchizedek now becomes a type of the Davidic king. The descendants of David will be kings and they will be priests; this is clearly expressed in 2 Samuel 8:18: "and David's sons were priests." This statement is very controversial and even the translations disagree on how to translate the word *kōhanîm* ("priests") in this section of the verse. The following translations translate the word *kōhanîm* in 2 Samuel 8:18 as "priests:" BBE, ESV, NAB, NET, NJB, RSV, NRSV, TNK, NEB, NIV 2011, and the TNIV. Other translations are not willing to accept the view that David's sons were priests. Instead, they reinterpret the word and say David's sons were his advisors. These are the ways the word *kōhanîm* is translated:

- Chief ministers: the ASV, JPS, NASB, and the NKJV.
- Chief officials: the HCSB.
- Chief rulers: the KJV, RWB, and the GNB.
- Princes: the DRA.
- Royal advisers: the NIV 1984.
- Priestly leaders: the NLT.
- Princes of the court: the Septuagint (LXX).

In defense of the translation of *kōhanîm* as "chief rulers" or "royal advisors," some commentators acknowledge the word *kōhen* means "priest," but that in early Israel the word was also used to designate a royal minister or a person who advised the king.

Keil, in order to justify translating the word *kōhanîm* as "confidants," cites 1 Kings 4:5, where Zabud, Nathan's son, is a *kōhen* ("priest") and "the king's friend," that is, the king's confidential advisor.[1]

Most of the translations that say David's sons were advisors base their translations on the interpretation offered by the Chronicler in 2 Chronicles 18:17 where David's sons are called "the chief officials in the service of the king." This description of the office occupied by David's sons reflects the post-exilic perspective of the Chronicler, where only Levites could serve as priests. Thus, the designation of David's sons as priests was unacceptable to the Chronicler.

Many English translations follow the Chronicler's unwillingness to acknowledge that individuals who were not Levites could become priests. Since the Chronicler does not use the word "priests," but calls the sons of David "chief officials at the king's side" (NIV), many English translations follow the reading of the Chronicler. But, as P. Kyle McCarter Jr. concluded: "Almost all critics, therefore, have agreed that the readings of I Chron 18:17 and the versions in II Sam 8:18 are interpretive paraphrases of the reading of MT by scribes who considered it impossible that there should be non-Levitical priests."[2]

In conclusion, it is better to translate the word *kōhanîm* as "priests" rather than "royal advisors." Since David performed some priestly functions in the Jerusalem cult, it is very possible he delegated some of his priestly responsibilities to his sons.

1. Keil, *The Books of Samuel*, 369.
2. McCarter Jr., *II Samuel*, 255.

22

"Him that Pisseth against the Wall"

IN HIS ARTICLE "'PISSER against a Wall': An Echo of Divination in Biblical Hebrew," Duane Smith draws on the language and culture of the ancient Near East in order to explain the meaning of a unique Hebrew expression, "him that pisseth against the wall."[1] This chapter will offer a few comments on some of the interpretations scholars have offered to interpret this colorful biblical phrase, evaluate Smith's proposal, and offer another possible way of understanding the meaning of the expression "him that pisseth against the wall."

The KJV uses very graphic and expressive language to translate a Hebrew phrase that most other English translations avoid translating it in its literal sense. The meaning of the phrase, "him that pisseth against the wall," is obscure and for this reason it has been interpreted differently by different scholars. It appears six times in the Hebrew Bible:

In 1 Samuel 25:22, the phrase appears in the context of David's threat against Nabal: "So and more also do God unto the enemies of David, if I leave of all that pertain to him by the morning light any that pisseth against the wall." In 1 Samuel 25:34, the phrase appears in the context of the reversal of David's threat against Nabal: "For in very deed, as the LORD God of Israel liveth, which hath kept me back from hurting thee, except thou hadst hasted and come to meet me, surely there had not been left unto Nabal by the morning light any that pisseth against the wall."

In 1 Kings 14:10, the phrase appears in the context of the words of judgment against the house of Jeroboam: "Therefore, behold, I will bring

1. Smith, "Pisser against a Wall," 699–717.

evil upon the house of Jeroboam, and will cut off from Jeroboam him that pisseth against the wall, and him that is shut up and left in Israel, and will take away the remnant of the house of Jeroboam, as a man taketh away dung, till it be all gone."

In 1 Kings 16:11, the phrase appears in the context of the words of judgment against the house of Baasha: "And it came to pass, when he began to reign, as soon as he sat on his throne, that he slew all the house of Baasha: he left him not one that pisseth against a wall, neither of his kinsfolks, nor of his friends." In 1 Kings 21:21, the phrase appears in the context of the words of judgment against the house of Ahab: "Behold, I will bring evil upon thee, and will take away thy posterity, and will cut off from Ahab him that pisseth against the wall, and him that is shut up and left in Israel." In 2 Kings 9:8, the phrase appears in the context of the words of judgment against the house of Ahab: "For the whole house of Ahab shall perish: and I will cut off from Ahab him that pisseth against the wall, and him that is shut up and left in Israel."

Most translations understand the phrase "him that pisseth against the wall" to refer to a man and translate the expression to describe a male descendant of the house being threatened. For instance, in the threat against the house of Jeroboam in 1 Kings 14:10, the NIV translates the phrase as "I will cut off from Jeroboam every last male in Israel—slave or free." The ASV translates the phrase as "I will cut off from Jeroboam every man-child." The NAB translates the phrase as "every male in Jeroboam's line."

In his article, Smith lists several proposals offered by scholars to interpret this obscure Hebrew expression. I cannot do justice to Smith's discussion of all the proposed interpretations offered by scholars. Those who are interested in reading the many views offered by scholars should consult Smith's article and follow his argument.

In short, most views can be grouped into four categories. First, the expression refers to males, men and boys or adult males of a family. Second, it means dogs as a pejorative for man. One scholar has interpreted the expression to refer to guard dogs or service dogs of the king. Third, the expression designates an evil person who deserves to be cut off from society. Fourth, the Talmud discusses the phrase in relation to the issue of whether it is permissible for a man to urinate on the side of another man's wall.

Smith's interpretation is based on the "urine omina" that appear in the Assyrian Dream Book. He suggests "him that pisseth against the wall" is "a person who hopes for progeny."[2] Smith's interpretation is unique. In his article, Smith studies the Assyrian urination omina and dream interpretation and how these urine omina help in understanding this mysterious Hebrew expression. Smith concludes that since the context in which this Hebrew expression is used refers to the elimination of progeny, then, in light of the urine omina, "him that pisseth against the wall" is "a person who hopes for progeny."[3] Smith's conclusion is based on solid research. Although there is some merit in Smith's proposal, his view that "him that pisseth against the wall" is a "person who hopes for progeny" does not fully explain the true meaning of the Hebrew expression.

Take, for instance, the case of David and Nabal (1 Sam 25). While David was living in Hebron, he and his men served as protectors of some of the landowners who lived in the area. One day when David and his army were in need of some food, he sent ten men to Nabal's house asking the rich landowner to give him some of his flock so he could feed his soldiers. Nabal refused David's request and offended David by calling him a runaway slave (1 Sam 25:10). David was irate, and in his anger made a solemn vow: "So and more also do God unto the enemies of David, if I leave of all that pertain to him by the morning light any that pisseth against the wall" (1 Sam 25:22 KJV).

There are two things in David's vow that militate against Smith's view. First, when David made his vow, his intention was to eliminate Nabal's house. David did not expect to kill men who hoped for progeny. He promised to kill every man in Nabal's house, young and old, thus eliminating from society the name of Nabal forever.

Second, from the context it is clear that Nabal had no idea that David had made a vow to eliminate the men in his house. The idea that the men in Nabal's house were hoping for progeny does not find support in the text. The same applies to the promises of judgment against the houses of Jeroboam, Baasha, and Ahab.

It is possible to say, as Smith writes in his article, that the Deuteronomistic redactors were familiar with the Akkadian urine omina, but it is doubtful that the redactors used the expression "him that pisseth against the wall" to refer to a person hoping for children in the future. One who reads the story of David and Nabal, either from David's perspective or from Nabal's perspective, will never conclude that "him that pisseth against the wall" means "a

2. Ibid., 700.
3. Ibid., 714.

person who hopes for progeny." The proper interpretation of the expression "him that pisseth against the wall" requires several clarifications of ideas implied in the text and a brief understanding of the cultural practices of Israel.

First, it is clear that the Hebrew expression "him that pisseth against the wall" contains a reference to dogs. This is how the Talmud understood this expression: "The meaning of the verse is this: 'Even a creature whose way is to piss against a wall I will not leave him. And what is this? A dog'" (*b. B. Bat.* 19b). Even Smith recognizes the allusion to dogs in this phrase. He writes: "Modern interpreters who follow this suggestion combine the empirical fact that male dogs do urinate against walls."[4] Second, this Hebrew expression is used pejoratively to describe men. This is the reason most English translations use a euphemism to translate the Hebrew expression. English translations use the word "male" to avoid using the expression "him that pisseth against the wall." The pejorative here conveys the idea "that some man [*sic*] is no better than a dog that urinates against a wall."[5] Third, in all the passages where the expression "him that pisseth against the wall" appears, the word "dog" also appears. For instance, in the case of Nabal, his behavior is compared to a dog. Hans W. Hertzberg, in his commentary on the book of Samuel translates 1 Samuel 25:3 as follows: "Now the name of the man was Nabal, and the name of his wife Abigail. The woman was of good understanding and beautiful, but the man was churlish and ill-behaved—a real Calebbite dog."[6] Nabal was from the house of Caleb, and Caleb in Hebrew means "dog." Dogs also appear in the words of judgment against Jeroboam: "Therefore, behold, I will bring evil upon the house of Jeroboam, and will cut off from Jeroboam him that pisseth against the wall, and him that is shut up and left in Israel, and will take away the remnant of the house of Jeroboam, as a man taketh away dung, till it be all gone. Him that dieth of Jeroboam in the city shall the dogs eat" (1 Kgs 14:10–11 KJV).

"Him that pisseth against the wall" and dogs also appear in the words of judgment against Baasha (1 Kgs 16:4; 16:11) and in the words of judgment against the house of Ahab (1 Kgs 21:21; 21:24; 2 Kgs 9:8; 9:10; 9:36). It is my firm conviction that the Hebrew expression "him that pisseth against the wall" must be understood in relation to how the people of Israel felt

---

4. Ibid., 703.

5. Ibid., 700.

6. Hertzberg, *I & II Samuel*, 199.

toward dogs. In Israel dogs were listed among the unclean animals because they ate the flesh of unclean animals (Exod 22:31).

In some societies of the ancient Near East, the word "dog" was used as a term of abuse. In the Old Testament, the word "dog" is used as a term of opprobrium. When the word is used to refer to a person, the use of the word represents a personal insult: "Then Abishai son of Zeruiah said to the king, 'Why should this dead dog curse my lord the king? Let me go over and take off his head'" (2 Sam 16:9). In Deuteronomy 23:19, the expression "wages of a dog" refers to the wages of a male prostitute.

The contempt expressed by the word "dog" is also applied to individuals. When the observable behavior of dogs was used to describe a person, it was considered the ultimate insult. For instance, the book of Proverbs says the fool is like the dog that returns to his vomit (Prov 26:11). This, then, brings us back to the Hebrew expression that has been the focus of this study. Ralph Klein, in his commentary on 1 Samuel called the expression "him that pisseth against the wall" vulgar language.[7] John Gray, in his commentary on 1–2 Kings said that this Hebrew expression "is a typical example of the direct, graphic, uninhibited speech of the Israelite peasant, particularly of the prophets."[8]

P. Kyle McCarter, in his commentary on 1 Samuel said this Hebrew expression is "a vulgarism that is appropriate on David's lips in his presumed state of mind."[9] G. J. Botterweck, in his discussion of the word "dog" in the Hebrew Bible, said "in the Hebrew Bible, portions of the canine anatomy are used to insult people."[10] In the passages listed above, the writers are using the action of a dog and applying it as an insult to refer to males. All the occurrences of the expression appear in contexts where people are angry or where one person threatens another person with extinction. When people are angry they use obscenity.

This Hebrew expression is an obscenity used to insult people. The common definition of obscenity is an expression that is used as an invective. In our society, the expression "him that pisseth against the wall" would be the equivalent to S.O.B. There are a few obscene expressions in the Hebrew Bible; "him that pisseth against the wall" is one of them.

---

7. Klein, *1 Samuel*, 23.

8. Gray, *I & II Kings*, 337.

9. McCarter, *I Samuel*, 398.

10. Botterweck, "*keleḇ*," in *TDOT* 7:153.

Some people may object and say the people of the Bible did not use obscenity, but the use of vulgar language is found in every culture, even in the culture of the people who constituted ancient Israel. Others may object that this obscenity appears in the mouth of kings and prophets. Since vulgar language is not commonly used in public, it is customary to use euphemisms to sanitize the language. John Milton, in his *An Apology for Smectymnuus*, was very critical of those who sanitize the rough language of the Bible. On the attempt to sanitize "him that pisseth against the wall," Milton wrote:

> Turn then to the First of Kings, where God himself uses the phrase, "I will cut off from Jeroboam him that pisseth against the wall"; which had it been an unseemly speech in the heat of an earnest expression, then we must conclude that Jonathan or Onkelos the targumists were of cleaner language than he that made the tongue; for they render it as briefly, "I will cut off all who are at years of discretion," that is to say, so much discretion as to hide nakedness. Whereas God, who is the author both of purity and eloquence, chose this phrase as fittest in that vehement character wherein he spake. Otherwise that plain word might have easily been forborne: which the mazoreths and rabbinical scholiasts, not well attending, have often used to blur the margin with Keri instead of Ketiv, and gave us this insulse rule out of their Talmud, "That all words which in the law are written obscenely, must be changed to more civil words": fools, who would teach men to read more decently than God thought good to write. And thus I take it to be manifest, that indignation against men and their actions notoriously bad hath leave and authority ofttimes to utter such words and phrases, as in common talk were not so mannerly to use.[11]

---

11. Milton, *Prose Works*, 84.

23

Whose Cloak Did Ahijah Tear?

THE PROPHET AHIJAH, A man from Shiloh, played an important role in the history of Israel. He appears only twice in the Old Testament and both times he speaks to Jeroboam, once to announce he would become king of the northern tribes and the other to announce his son would die. The purpose of this chapter is to discuss Ahijah's role in the division of the kingdom after Solomon's death and the selection of Jeroboam to become the king of the Northern Kingdom.

The division of the united monarchy occurred because of Solomon's rejection of God and his promotion of pagan practices in Jerusalem. The book of Kings presents a very negative view of Solomon's religious practices:

> For when Solomon was old, his wives turned away his heart after other gods; and his heart was not true to the LORD his God, as was the heart of his father David. For Solomon followed Astarte the goddess of the Sidonians, and Milcom the abomination of the Ammonites. So Solomon did what was evil in the sight of the LORD, and did not completely follow the LORD, as his father David had done. Then Solomon built a high place for Chemosh the abomination of Moab, and for Molech the abomination of the Ammonites, on the mountain east of Jerusalem (1 Kgs 11:4–7).

The Bible says that "the LORD was angry with Solomon, because his heart had turned away from the LORD, the God of Israel" (1 Kgs 11:9). As a result of Solomon's sins, the Lord raised three "satans" against Solomon: Hadad the Edomite (1 Kgs 11:14), Rezon of Damascus (1 Kgs 11:23), and Jeroboam, the son of Nebat, an Ephraimite from Zeredah, a servant of Solomon (1 Kgs 11:26).

The word "satan" is translated "adversary" in most English Bibles. The word "satan" refers to someone who becomes the adversary of another person. In this case, the satans or the adversaries were individuals whom God used to punish Solomon for his unfaithfulness.

The announcement of the division of the kingdom of Israel came through Ahijah. In his announcement, Ahijah told Jeroboam the kingdom would be divided. However, the house of David would continue over two tribes as a fulfillment of God's covenant with David. God had promised David he would not remove the kingdom from his son as he had removed the kingdom from Saul.

God's covenant with David included a promise of continuity of his dynasty: "When he commits iniquity, I will punish him with a rod such as mortals use, with blows inflicted by human beings. But I will not take my steadfast love from him, as I took it from Saul . . . Your house and your kingdom shall be made sure forever before me; your throne shall be established forever" (2 Sam 7:14–16).

Ahijah was a prophet from Shiloh. In the days of the judges, Shiloh was the place where the sanctuary of the Lord was located and the place where the Ark of the Covenant was housed. During the days of Eli and Samuel, the sanctuary at Shiloh was destroyed and the Ark was captured by the Philistines (1 Sam 4:1–11).

It is possible the religious leaders who were from Shiloh resented the many religious innovations introduced by Solomon into the religious life of the nation. They also opposed the building of places of worship for the foreign gods Solomon erected in Jerusalem. Ahijah's sentiment reflects the general opposition the people of the North had for the Davidic monarchy (2 Sam 20:1). This is the reason Ahijah approached Jeroboam and told him about God's decision.

Jeroboam was a supervisor in Solomon's work force: "Jeroboam was very able, and when Solomon saw that the young man was industrious he gave him charge over all the forced labor of the house of Joseph" (1 Kgs 11:28). While Jeroboam was preparing to inspect the work, Ahijah met him as he was leaving Jerusalem, probably after Jeroboam had a meeting with the king and after he was installed into his position as overseer of all the work given to the sons of Joseph.

During this meeting Ahijah told Jeroboam that he would lead a revolt against Solomon and that he would become the leader of the northern tribes. To dramatize his oracle, Ahijah took a cloak and tore it into twelve pieces.

Ahijah gave ten pieces to Jeroboam and said: "Take for yourself ten pieces; for thus says the LORD, the God of Israel, 'See, I am about to tear the kingdom from the hand of Solomon, and will give you ten tribes'" (1 Kgs 11:31).

The tearing of the cloak into twelve pieces was significant because it represented the twelve tribes of Israel, all the people of God. The tearing of the cloak also indicates the kingdom would be divided into two kingdoms with their own political and religious traditions. Ahijah's symbolic action was an affirmation that Jeroboam was the individual chosen by God to humble Rehoboam, Solomon's son.

The news of what Ahijah had done probably spread fast because Solomon was told of Ahijah's words and the planned revolt. Because of this conspiracy against his kingdom, Solomon sought to kill Jeroboam: "Solomon sought therefore to kill Jeroboam; but Jeroboam promptly fled to Egypt, to King Shishak of Egypt, and remained in Egypt until the death of Solomon" (1 Kgs 11:40).

The events that led to the division of the kingdom are evident. What is not evident is whose cloak Ahijah tore. Even the different English versions of 1 Kings 11:29 are ambivalent on this issue. For instance, the NRSV translates 1 Kings 11:29 as follows: "About that time, when Jeroboam was leaving Jerusalem, the prophet Ahijah the Shilonite found him on the road. Ahijah had clothed himself with a new garment."

On the other hand, the NIV translates the same verse as follows: "About that time Jeroboam was going out of Jerusalem, and Ahijah the prophet of Shiloh met him on the way, wearing a new cloak." The NRSV says Ahijah was wearing the cloak while the NIV does not say who was wearing the cloak. The fact is the name Ahijah, as in "Ahijah had clothed himself with a new garment," is not in the Hebrew. The Hebrew says "And he was wearing a new cloak," without saying who "he" was.

In their commentary on 2 Kings, Cogan and Tadmor write: "Jeroboam was wearing the cloak. The wording of the succeeding clause, 'took hold of, grabbed' solves the ambiguousness of this clause, because this action is inappropriate on one's own garment; rather the action was performed on a garment worn by a second party (cf. Gen 39:12). Thus, Ahijah seized Jeroboam's cloak."[1] Cogan and Tadmor say the Hebrew word *wayyitpōs* is also used in the story of Joseph when Potiphar's wife seized Joseph's garment. Thus, the word is generally used when someone takes hold of something

---

1. Cogan and Tadmor, *II Kings*, 339.

that belongs to another. In this case, it is Ahijah who takes hold of the cloak that belonged to Jeroboam.

The addition made by most versions of the name Ahijah into the clause is an attempt at solving the ambiguity of the text, but this attempt creates a false interpretation of what happened in the meeting between Ahijah and Jeroboam. Jeroboam probably received his new garment during his meeting with Solomon. Ahijah's encounter with Jeroboam came immediately after Jeroboam left Jerusalem. It is possible the cloak was his new official garment symbolizing his authority as the new officer over the house of Joseph (1 Kgs 11:28).

It was for the sake of David that God allowed Rehoboam to be king of Judah after Solomon's death. Solomon had not kept the terms of the covenant God established with his father David. The garment Solomon gave to Jeroboam, his officer, to signify his authority over the northern tribes, was used as a prophetic symbolism to announce the division of the kingdom and the punishment of Solomon for his unfaithfulness.

24

The Challenges of Parenthood

THERE ARE MANY GENEALOGIES in the Old Testament. The first nine chapters of 1 Chronicles are composed of a series of genealogies. Most people who regularly read the Bible generally skip these genealogies because they are boring to read. It is true a simple list of names may be irrelevant to many, but these genealogies display the complicated relationships between distant generations and provide important information about the facts and circumstances related to the members of a family. Although bare names in a genealogy may be insignificant to a casual reader, to an attentive reader genealogies teach important historical lessons and other truths that may not have been intended by the original writer.

The genealogies that appear in the Old Testament, in general, are related to the ancestors of Israel. At times, the names may refer to father and son or they may refer to distant ancestors or different generations. The genealogies served to reinforce the sense of kinship among members of a clan. The genealogies also promoted nationalistic feelings that served to connect an individual with the traditions of the past. In the genealogy of the kings of Judah that appears in the gospel of Matthew, we learn a great lesson. "Uzziah was the father of Jotham. Jotham was the father of Ahaz. Ahaz was the father of Hezekiah. Hezekiah was the father of Manasseh. Manasseh was the father of Amon. Amon was the father of Josiah" (Matt 1:9–10 NLT). Uzziah was the father of Jotham: a good king is the father of a good king. This is not unexpected because, generally, a good father will become the father of a good son. Jotham was the father of Ahaz: a good king becomes the father of an evil king. This is disappointing, for a good father expects his son to be a good son and follow his example.

Ahaz was the father of Hezekiah: an evil king becomes the father of one of the best kings of Judah. Now, that is a blessing because we learn children do not have to follow the evil ways of their parents. Hezekiah was the father of Manasseh: one of the best kings of Judah becomes the father of the worst king of Judah. Now, that is a mystery, for how can the goodness of a good father not affect the life of his son? The fact is children make their own decisions and choose a life for themselves, even when that life is evil.

Manasseh was the father of Amon: an evil king becomes the father of an evil king. This also is not unexpected, because at times, sons follow the evil example of their fathers. Amon was the father of Josiah: an evil king becomes the father of the best king of Judah. This clearly shows children do not have to follow the evil example of their fathers. There is a lesson all of us must learn from this genealogy: It is tough being a parent. As we look at this genealogy, we learn a person's relationship with another person in a genealogy may be complicated. For instance, a trait that appears in the life of a man may appear also in the life of his son or grandson. In the same way, the presence of a trait in a child may not be a characteristic found in the life of either parent. One good example of this principle is found in the following quotation from Thomas Fuller, the seventeenth century theologian:

> Lord, I find the genealogy of my Saviour strangely checkered with four remarkable changes in four immediate generations:
>
> 1. Rehoboam begat Abiam; that is, a bad father begat a bad son.
> 2. Abiam begat Asa; that is, a bad father a good son.
> 3. Asa begat Jehoshaphat; that is, a good father a good son.
> 4. Jehoshaphat begat Joram; a good father a bad son.
>
> I see, Lord, from hence that my father's piety cannot be entailed; that is bad news for me. But I see also that actual impiety is not always hereditary; that is good news for my son.[1]

Joy and happiness, disappointment and pain are some of the experiences parents have to face in the rearing of their children. As children grow up, parents take great satisfaction in the accomplishments of their children, but they also experience the pains and disappointments that come as the children fail their parents' expectations. Joy and disappointments come with the agony and the ecstasy of being parents.

---

1. Fuller, *Writings*, 50–51.

Parents hurt when they believe they have failed in their God-given task of bringing their children to love and obey God. Parents hurt when their children reject the moral values or standards they worked so hard to instill in the lives of their children. When crises arrive, parents blame themselves for failing to provide a good education for their children. They judge themselves for their failure and feel guilty because they cannot understand what went wrong. But, in order for them to deal with their sense of failure, they must understand the lesson Ezekiel teaches: "A child shall not suffer for the iniquity of a parent, nor a parent suffer for the iniquity of a child; the righteousness of the righteous shall be his own, and the wickedness of the wicked shall be his own" (Ezek 18:20).

SECTION THREE

Wisdom and Poetical Books

25

Psalm 8:5: In Search of a Better Translation

PSALM 8 IS A hymn of praise in which the psalmist celebrates God's majesty in creation and the dignity of every human being. In awe and amazement, the psalmist proclaims the majesty of God as the creator of the universe. Impressed by the transcendence of the Creator, the psalmist becomes aware of the smallness and insignificance of every human being. The psalmist also recognizes human beings have been favored by God. Aware of the honor God has placed on human beings, in awe, the psalmist asks: "What is man, that thou art mindful of him? And the son of man, that thou visitest him? For thou hast made him a little lower than the angels, and hast crowned him with glory and honour" (Ps 8:4–5 KJV).

The words of the psalmist address the place of human beings in God's creation. The crowning of human beings with honor reflects the idea of dominion over God's creation, which is clearly present in Genesis 1:26–28, a text where God places human beings over all created things. The words of verse 5 have been translated in several different ways, causing some confusion in the minds of lay people who read Psalm 8 in different translations. In this study, I propose to look at the meaning of Psalm 8:5 and suggest which translation is a better reading of the Hebrew text.

The KJV translates the Hebrew word *ĕlōhîm* as "angels." The following English translations also translate *'ĕlōhîm* as "angels": the CJB, the DBY, the DRA, the NIV 2011, the JPS, the NKJV, and the RWB. The BBE translates the Hebrew phrase as follows: "a little lower than the gods." The ESV, the NET, the NIV 1984, and the TNIV translate as follows: "a little lower than the heavenly beings." The NAB translates as follows: "a little lower than a god." The NJB translates as follows: "a little less than a god." The TNK translates as follows: "A little less than divine." The YLT translates as follows: "[Thou] causest him to lack a little of Godhead." The ASV, the ERV, the GNB, the NASB, the NLT, and the NRSV translate as follows: "A little lower than God." The HCSB and the RSV translate as follows: "a little less than God." The GWN and the CEV translate: "a little lower than yourself."

These different translations reflect the problem translators have in understanding what the psalmist was trying to convey to his audience. This problem was already present in the early versions. For instance, the Septuagint (the Greek translation of the Old Testament), the Peshitta (the Aramaic version of the Old Testament), and the Vulgate (the Latin version of the Bible) understood the Hebrew word *ĕlōhîm* to mean "angels" and through the Septuagint, this translation has entered many English versions. Even in the New Testament, the author of Hebrews 2:7, when talking about the nature of Christ, did not quote from the Hebrew text of Psalm 8:5, but quoted from the Septuagint to describe the humiliation of Christ.

In order to ascertain which translation reflects a better understanding of the Hebrew text, it becomes important to understand the words of the psalmist. In Psalm 8, the psalmist is writing about the role human beings play in God's creation. The psalmist believes human beings share in the nature of God. Men and women were created in the image and likeness of God (Gen 1:26–27), and therefore they are like God himself.

Thus, the psalmist used the word *ĕlōhîm* to describe one aspect of human nature. The word *ĕlōhîm* never appears in the Old Testament, meaning "angel." The Septuagint translates *ĕlōhîm* as "angels" in Psalm 97:7; 138:1. However, most English translations do not follow the Septuagint here.

For instance, the NRSV translates the second part of Psalm 97:7 as follows: "all gods bow down before him." The TNK translates as follows: "all divine beings bow down to Him." However, the DRB, following the Vulgate and the Septuagint, translates Psalm 97:7 as follows: "Adore him, all you his angels." As for Psalm 138:1, both the NJB and the DRB follow the Septuagint and translate the word *ĕlōhîm* as "angels." The word *ĕlōhîm* means "God" or "gods." Thus, the psalmist is emphasizing that human beings were created in the image and likeness of God and by nature, they are a little less than God himself.

Peter C. Craigie, in his commentary on the book of Psalms, writes: "The translation *angel* may have been prompted by modesty, for it may have seemed rather extravagant to claim that mankind was only a little less than God. Nevertheless, the translation *God* is almost certainly correct, and the words probably contain an allusion to the image of God in mankind and the God-given role of dominion to be exercised by mankind within the created order."[1] Thus, there is no doubt a better translation of the Hebrew phrase should avoid the words "angels" or "divine beings." Human beings were created "a little lower than God." The psalmist is aware that human beings have a special relationship with God, because, in addition to being created in the image and likeness of God, human beings play a special role in God's creation.

"When I look at your heavens, the work of your fingers, the moon and the stars that you have established; what are human beings that you are mindful of them, mortals that you care for them? Yet you have made them a little lower than God, and crowned them with glory and honor" (Ps 8:3–5 NRSV). Thus, the better translation of Psalm 8:5 should affirm that human beings were created "a little lower than God."

---

1. Craigie, *Psalms*, 108.

26

Understanding Psalm 17:14

THE PROPER UNDERSTANDING OF Psalm 17:14 is very difficult because English translations differ on whether the ones who receive God's blessings are the wicked or the righteous. An explanation of this passage requires a discussion and exegesis of the Hebrew text and an evaluation of how the translations have approached the text. In order to understand the meaning and the message of the text, I will show how different English translations of the Bible have translated this difficult passage.

The HCSV translates Psalm 17:14 as follows: "With Your hand, LORD, save me from men, from men of the world, whose portion is in this life: You fill their bellies with what You have in store, their sons are satisfied, and they leave their surplus to their children." The ESV translates as follows: "from men by your hand, O LORD, from men of the world whose portion is in this life. You fill their womb with treasure; they are satisfied with children, and they leave their abundance to their infants." The GWN translates as follows: "With your power rescue me from mortals, O LORD, from mortals who enjoy their inheritance only in this life. You fill their bellies with your treasure. Their children are satisfied with it, and they leave what remains to their children." The KJV translates as follows: "From men which are thy hand, O LORD, from men of the world, which have their portion in this life, and whose belly thou fillest with thy hid treasure: they are full of children, and leave the rest of their substance to their babes."

In addition, the Septuagint (LXX) translates as follows: "because of the enemies of thine hand: O Lord, destroy them from the earth; scatter them in their life, though their belly has been filled with thy hidden treasures: they have been satisfied with uncleanness, and have left the remnant of their possessions to their babes." The NIV translates as follows: "By your hand save me from such people, LORD, from those of this world whose reward is in this life. May what you have stored up for the wicked fill their bellies; may their children gorge themselves on it, and may there be leftovers for their little ones." The NRSV translates as follows: "from mortals—by your hand, O LORD—from mortals whose portion in life is in this world. May their bellies be filled with what you have stored up for them; may their children have more than enough; may they leave something over to their little ones." The TNK translates as follows: "from men, O LORD, with Your hand, from men whose share in life is fleeting. But as to Your treasured ones, fill their bellies. Their sons too shall be satisfied, and have something to leave over for their young."

It is clear from these different translations of Psalm 17:14 that scholars differ in their understanding of what the psalmist was trying to communicate to his readers. There are two important issues of interpretation that make the proper translation of verse 14 difficult. First, in order to solve the double occurrence of the word "men" in the verse, many scholars have decided to emend the text. For instance, Hans-Joachim Kraus translates the first part of verse 14 as follows: "May a cruel death at your hand, O Yahweh, / a cruel death put an end to their portion in life!"[1] Michael Dahood translates verse 14a as follows: "Slay them with your hand, O Yahweh, / slay them from the earth, / Make them perish from among the living!"[2]

I do not think it is necessary to emend the text to gain the proper meaning of the text. If one takes verse 14 as a continuation of the argument advanced in 13, then the text makes sense without radical emendation: "Arise, O LORD! confront them, overthrow them! Deliver my life from the wicked by your sword, [deliver me] from men by your hand, O LORD, from men whose portion in life is of the world." Thus the psalmist is asking the Lord himself to deliver him from the power of the wicked. The expression "deliver me" in verse 13 should also be understood at the beginning of 14.

Another possibility is to take the duplicate occurrence of the word "men" (*meṯim*) in its consonantal form and repoint the two words as a Hiphil Participle from מות (*mûṯ*, "cause to die," "kill"). This alternative follows the translation present in the Septuagint. This is the view taken by Dahood (see above) and Craigie: "Kill them by your hand O Lord, / Kill them from the

---

1. Kraus, *Psalms 1–59*, 244.
2. Dahood, *Psalms 1–50*, 93.

world."[3] Both options make good sense in the context of the whole psalm. I prefer to retain the reading of the Hebrew Bible without repointing the text.

The second issue that complicates the translation of verse 14 is whose belly God is filling. The decision of whose belly is being filled depends on whether the translation follows the *ketiv* (the word *ketiv* indicates the written form of the text) or the *qere* (the word *qere* indicates how the word should be read). Translators who adopt the *ketiv* understand the filled belly is the belly of the wicked: "May their bellies be filled with what you have stored up for them" (NRSV). Translators who adopt the *qere* understand the filled belly is the belly of the righteous: "But as to Your treasured ones, fill their bellies" (TNK). God's people are called "Your treasured ones." Therefore, the translation that sees God blessing the righteous may be a better understanding of the text. Thus, Psalm 17:13–14 should be translated as follows: "Arise, O LORD! confront them, overthrow them! Deliver my life from the wicked by your sword, [deliver me] from men by your hand, O LORD, from men whose portion in life is of the world. As for your treasured ones, you will fill their belly. Their children will have more than enough."

Psalm 17 is the prayer of one oppressed and persecuted by wicked people, one who is aware of his righteousness before God. This individual approached God in prayer and asked to be vindicated. The psalmist asked for protection against wicked people whose reward is in this world. In his declaration of praise, the psalmist recognized God blesses the righteous and provides for their children.

3. Craigie, *Psalms 1–50*, 160.

27

Jezebel's Wedding Song

PSALM 45 IS AN epithalamium, a wedding song. Long before scholars began classifying the Psalms according to form, scholars had already concluded that Psalm 45 was a wedding song composed to celebrate a royal wedding. Psalm 45 is a love song (v. 1) composed for a special event, which, according to the text, was an event that occurred in the days of the writer. This love song was probably sung during the marriage ceremony of one of the kings of Judah or Israel. Psalm 45 is divided into four sections:

a. *The introduction*: In the introduction, the poet describes the purpose of his song (v. 1).

b. *An address to the groom*: This section praises the king and describes the noble character of the king as a ruler whose kingship has been approved by God (vv. 2–9).

c. *An address to the bride*: This section exhorts the bride to accept the king, describes her wardrobe, the wedding procession, and introduces the queen's companions (vv. 10–15).

d. *An address to the groom*: This section speaks of the king's heirs and their glorious future (vv. 16–17).

The purpose of this chapter is to identify the groom and the bride and apply the words of Psalm 45 to the wedding ceremony. The study begins with an identification of the main characters mentioned in the psalm.

The Scribe

The composer of this psalm describes himself as a *sôphēr māhîr*, a skilled scribe. In antiquity, kings employed scribes because of their ability to write. Scribes were employed to prepare legal documents and keep records of business transactions. In Israel, kings also had scribes at their service (2 Sam 8:17). However, since the writer says his tongue is like the pen of a scribe, it is possible the writer is a poet who presented his composition orally.

The author of Psalm 45 was employed to compose a song to celebrate the wedding of the king and his bride. The poet used exalted language to describe the king: "My heart is moved by a noble theme as I compose my song for the king." The singer addresses the king as God (v. 6), as one who possesses all the qualities of the ideal king, as a conqueror who sits on a throne of righteousness, and as a groom dressed in splendor.

The Groom

The identity of the king is not revealed in the text. Several kings of Judah and Israel have been identified as the king to whom this wedding song was dedicated.

1. Some commentators identify the king with the Messiah. Those who advocate the messianic interpretation of Psalm 45 apply the language of the psalm to describe Christ's relationship with his church. The quotation of Psalm 45:6–7 by the writer of the book of Hebrews (Heb 1:8–9) reinforces the messianic interpretation of the text. The messianic interpretation is weakened by the fact that the language of the psalm does not describe the future glory of the Messiah.

2. Some commentators believe the groom was Solomon. If the king was Solomon, then the bride was either pharaoh's daughter (1 Kgs 11:1), the daughter of Hiram, king of Tyre (1 Kgs 5:1), or the Sidonian woman mentioned in 1 Kings 11:1. However, the description of the king as a warrior does not fit Solomon, who was known as a man of peace.

3. Franz Delitzsch believed the king was Joram, the son of Jehoshaphat, and the bride was Athaliah, the daughter of Ahab and granddaughter of Omri. The reason for this identification is because Delitzsch believed the exalted language used to describe the king could only refer to a descendant of David and be related to God's promise to David in

2 Samuel 7.[1] The problem with Delitzsch's interpretation is the fact that, if Athaliah was the daughter of Ahab and Jezebel,[2] then she was born in Israel and not in Tyre, although the mention of Tyre could be a reference to the Tyrian origin of Jezebel, Athaliah's mother.

4. H. Ewald believed the king mentioned in the Psalm was Jeroboam II because the language of the psalm refers to a king of the Northern Kingdom, since the Northern Kingdom had a closer relationship with Tyre. The queen was not Jezebel because homage to the queen is to come to her from Tyre.[3]

5. A few commentators believe the king mentioned in the psalm was David. However, this interpretation has little merit because of the many wives of David mentioned in 2 Samuel 3:2–5 and 5:13, none of them were from Tyre.

6. H. Schmidt believed the mention of the "people of Tyre" in verse 12 points to Jezebel, Ahab's wife.[4] In addition, the mention of ivory palaces and stringed instruments in verse 8 points to Ahab and not Solomon (see 1 Kgs 22:39; Amos 3:15).

Most commentators reject the view that the king mentioned in Psalm 45 was Ahab, the son of Omri, king of Israel. The reason for this rejection is based primarily on the use of the exalted language used to describe the king. Since the king is addressed as God in verse 6 and since the language of the psalm is assumed to be messianic, commentators say only a descendant of David could fit the language used by the scribe to describe the king. Thus, scholars lean toward the Messiah (Christ), David, Solomon, and even Joram.

Ahab fits the description of the king mentioned in the psalm. There are at least three reasons to believe Ahab was the king whose wedding is being celebrated in Psalm 45:

1. Ahab married Jezebel, the daughter of Ethbaal, king of the Sidonians (1 Kgs 16:31).

2. Ahab built an ivory palace (or a place inlaid with ivory, cf. 1 Kgs 22:39; Amos 3:15), while Solomon only had a throne of ivory (1 Kgs 10:18).

---

1. Delitzsch, *Commentary on the Psalms*, 75–76.

2. 2 Kgs 8:18 and 2 Chr 21:6 say Athaliah was the daughter of Ahab; 2 Kgs 8:26 and 2 Chr 22:2 say Athaliah was the daughter of Omri.

3. Ewald, *Commentary on the Psalms*, 1:169.

4. Schmidt, H. *Die Psalmen*, 87.

3. Ahab was a warrior whose soldiers and chariots confronted Shalmaneser III and the Assyrian army in the battle of Qarqar on the Orontes.

The psalmist uses vivid language to describe the splendor of the king and the queen. The following description of the king and the queen is a compilation of several translations of the Psalm 45.

The Splendor of the King

1. His beauty: "You are the most handsome of men."

2. His gracious words: "Grace flows from your lips."

3. His courage in battle: "Mighty warrior, strap your sword at your side."

4. His administration of justice: "Ride on in majesty to victory for the defense of truth and justice."

5. His victory in wars: "May your right hand win you great victories. May your arrows pierce the hearts of the king's enemies; may the nations fall under your feet."

6. The stability of his kingdom: "Your throne, God, is forever and ever."

7. The righteousness of his kingdom: "The scepter of your kingdom is a scepter of justice. You love righteousness and hate what is evil."

8. His divine gifts: "God, your God, has anointed you, more than any other king."

9. The splendor of his reign: "Myrrh, aloes, and cassia perfume all your garments; from ivory palaces harps bring you joy."

The Glories of the Queen

1. Her attendants: "Kings's daughters and honorable women."

2. Her dignity: "A king's daughter."

3. Her title: "The Queen."

4. Her honor: "The bride of the king."

5. Her place of honor: "She stands on the right hand of the king."

6. Her wardrobe: "Dressed with gold of Ophir."

7. Her appearance: "Glorious in her golden gown."

8. Her sacrifice: "Forget your people and your father's house."

9. Her reward: "Your royal husband delights in your beauty."

The Wedding Song

Dedication

My heart is moved by a noble theme
as I compose my song for the king;
my tongue is the pen of a skillful writer.

To the King

You are the most handsome of men; grace flows from your lips.
Therefore God has blessed you forever.
Mighty warrior, strap your sword at your side.
You are so glorious, so majestic.
Ride on in majesty to victory for the defense of truth and justice.
May your right hand win you great victories.
May your arrows pierce the hearts of the king's enemies;
may the nations fall under your feet.
Your throne, God, is forever and ever;
the scepter of your kingdom is a scepter of justice.
You love righteousness and hate what is evil;
therefore God, your God, has anointed you,
more than any other king, with the oil of joy.
Myrrh, aloes, and cassia perfume all your garments;
from ivory palaces harps bring you joy.
Kings's daughters are among your honored women;
the queen stands at your right hand, adorned with gold from Ophir.

To the Bride

Bride of the king, listen to me,
forget your people and your father's house,
for your royal husband delights in your beauty.
Honor him, for he is your lord.

The people of Tyre will bring you gifts,
rich people will try to win your favor.
In her palace the queen looks glorious in her golden gown.
In her colorful gown she is led to the king,
followed by her bridesmaids,
and they also are brought to the king.
They enter the king's palace with gladness and rejoicing.

To the King

You, my king, will have many sons
to succeed your ancestors as kings,
and you will make them rulers over the whole earth.
My song will keep your name alive forever,
and everyone will praise you for all time to come.

28

Psalm 100:3: In Search of a Better Translation

PSALM 100 IS ONE of those great psalms of the Bible. The psalm is a song of thanksgiving, calling all people to praise God as the creator of the universe. All nations are invited to serve the Lord because of his goodness and faithfulness. The doctrine of creation in the Old Testament was Israel's testimony of the uniqueness and sovereignty of the God of Israel over nations and individuals. In the very act of creation, God demonstrates his power by calling the world into existence. Thus, in his call for human beings to worship God, the psalmist declares we are not self-created; we owe our existence to God, because only the God of Israel is the creator: "Know ye that the Lord is God: it is he that hath made us, and not we ourselves; we are his people, and the sheep of his pasture" (Psalm 100:3 KJV).

The translation of the King James Version poses a difficult issue of interpretation. The problem is focused on a textual corruption introduced into the Hebrew text. In Hebrew, there are several words that sound alike but have different meanings. Words that sound alike are called homophones. A homophone is "a word pronounced the same as, but differing in meaning from another, whether spelled the same way or not, as in 'heir' and 'air.'"[1] There are many homophones in English also; a classical example of a homophone is found in the words "aye," "eye," and "I."

In biblical Hebrew there are many words pronounced the same but have different meanings. Two of them are the word *lo'* (Hebrew לֹא) and the word *lô* (Hebrew לוֹ). The first word is negative and means "not." The second word is positive and means "to him."

---

1. "Homophone," *The Random House Dictionary*, 686.

In Psalm 100:3 the written Hebrew text or the *ketiv* (the word *ketiv* means "what is written") reads *lo'*, "not." However, an old scribal tradition notes in the margin of the text that the correct reading of the text should be *lô*, "to him." This marginal reading is called the *qere*. The word *qere* means "what should be read." In making this marginal note, the scribe or scribes who copied the text are telling the reader that even though the text reads *lo'*, "not," that it should be read *lô*, "to him."

Several older translations have adopted what is written in the text. Among these are the DBY, the DRA, the GBV, the KJV, the NASB, the NKJV, and the RWB. Modern translations, such the NIV, the ESV, and others, have adopted the correction proposed by the scribes. For instance, the NRSV: "Know that the LORD is God. It is he that made us, and we are his; we are his people, and the sheep of his pasture."

In light of the different readings between the older and modern translations, which translation is better? Which translation provides a better understanding of what the psalmist was trying to convey to his readers? As it is, both translations are plausible and both of them make sense. Both readings would fit the context of the words of the psalmist and both readings would be in harmony with the teachings of the Old Testament.

The reading of the KJV is found also in the Septuagint (the Greek version of the Old Testament), the Vulgate (the Latin version of the Bible), and the Peshitta (the Aramaic version of the Old Testament). However, from the perspective of the world of the Old Testament and of other nations in the ancient Near East, no people of antiquity, however primitive they might have been, believed they had made themselves. Only someone with a sense of grandeur, one who is obsessed with the pride of possession, one who would believe himself to be a god, like the pharaoh of Egypt, would dare say about a small part of creation: "The Nile is mine, and I have made it for myself" (Ezek 29:3). Every Israelite believed the Lord to be the true creator. The faith of Israel declared men and women derived their beings from God. A similar idea to Psalm 100:3 is also found in Psalm 95:7: "For he is our God, and we are the people of his pasture, and the sheep of his hand."

The message of Psalm 100:3 is clear: God is the creator. He made us, therefore, we are not independent, but belong to him. For this reason, the reading of the NRSV and other modern translations should be adopted. Because God created us and because we belong to him, we should worship the Lord with gladness, we should come into his presence with singing (Ps 100:2). The difference between the KJV and modern translations raises an important issue to readers of the Bible: Which version is better? The answer to this question requires a brief explanation of what is involved in dealing with textual problems in the Old Testament and how the scribes knew errors of transmission had crept into the biblical text. The scribes who copied the text of the Old Testament were called the Sopherim, "Men of the Book." Their main responsibility was to copy the manuscripts and make sure they were preserved for posterity.

Another group of scribes was called the Masoretes. The Masoretes transmitted the traditional reading of the text, counted the number of words and letters in the different books of the Hebrew Bible, and catalogued the errors found in the text. This is the reason the text of the Hebrew Bible is called "The Masoretic Text." In addition, the notes and information placed on the margins of the Hebrew Bible are called "The Masorah." The word "Masorah" means "tradition."

Describing the work of the Masoretes, Norman K. Gottwald, in his book *The Hebrew Bible*, writes: "Included in the marginal and final Masorah was a great mass of technical information and instruction that served to alert copyists to the minutest details and peculiarities of the text so that they might be copied with unfailing accuracy. The Masoretic notes identified unusual spellings, words, and grammatical forms, and often took account of their frequency of occurrence and exact locations throughout the biblical text."[2] Because the Masoretes knew the text and the sounds of the words by memory and because they transmitted the traditional reading of the biblical text from generation to generation, it was easy for them to notice an error in transmission. This is what happened with Psalm 100:3. According to the Masoretes, there are fifteen places in the Old Testament where the problem with the homophone containing the word *lô* (Hebrew לוֹ) and the word *lo'* (Hebrew לֹא) appear.

As for which version is better, it is important to remember all translations are good, but some translations may translate a verse or a word better than others. Some versions attempt to translate the Bible in today's English, since the "thees" and "thous" of the KJV are hardly used today. The Bible is the word of God and no textual problem, error in transmission, or language used will change that. God's word was written to help believers know God and his divine plan for humanity. Thus, every Bible, no matter what translation is used, will help readers know what God has accomplished in the history of Israel and in Jesus Christ.

2. Gottwald, *The Hebrew Bible*, 119.

Biblical scholars and Old Testament professors may debate how to translate a word in the Bible or how to understand a text in a biblical book. They also may debate the original text or the original intent of a biblical writer. This is the reason biblical scholars write so many books, and at times, why they cannot agree on their final conclusions. The average person, however, desires mostly to discover God's will for his or her life and how to live according to God's teachings. This can be accomplished by studying God's word in the KJV, the ESV, the NRSV, or in any other version.

It is for this reason students of the Bible should not allow the different versions to confuse or scare them. In the end, those who love the Bible should remember this: The Bible is the word of God, no matter what version one uses and no matter what textual problems may be present in a text of Scripture.

29

Sons or Children?

PSALM 127 IS A wisdom psalm in which the psalmist wants to teach that all human efforts are in vain if they lack divine blessing. Only God can assure prosperity and blessing. Psalm 127 can be divided into two sections. The first section (vv. 1–2) shows that only God gives success to human enterprise. The psalmist's words speak of the futility of human efforts when these efforts are devoid of God's blessings. An individual may build a house, but he may not be sure he will dwell in it. Deuteronomy 28:30 speaks of the curses that will come upon Israel when the people violate the demands of the covenant: "You shall become engaged to a woman, but another man shall lie with her. You shall build a house, but not live in it. You shall plant a vineyard, but not enjoy its fruit" (cf. also Zeph 1:13). A watchman watching over a city may sound the alarm at the approach of danger (Ezek 3:17), but he many not prevent the attack of an enemy. In the second section, (vv. 3–5) the psalmist says that sons are a blessing from God. For the Israelites, a family with many sons was one of the greatest demonstrations of divine favor: "And Obed-edom had [eight] sons . . . for God blessed him" (1 Chron 26:4–5).

People in Israel believed all things came from God, including sons, since they were seen as God's gift, especially the sons of one's youth, be-cause they are strong and because they are the firstfruits of one's strength (Gen 49:3). So, when the psalmist declared how blessed he was, he wrote: "Sons are indeed a heritage from the LORD, the fruit of the womb a reward. Like arrows in the hand of a warrior are the sons of one's youth. Happy is the man who has his quiver full of them. He shall not be put to shame when he speaks with his enemies in the gate" (Ps 127:3–5).

The versions are not unanimous in translating Psalm 127:3. A survey of twenty-eight translations of Psalm 127:3 reveal the following results: ten versions, including the NRSV, the NJB, and the NIV 1984, have "sons." Eighteen versions, including the ESV, the NIV 2011, and the TNIV have "children." If these translations differ in their understanding of whether Psalm 127:3 should be translated "sons" or "children," then, which translation is better? Are the translations that use "sons" misleading the readers? Is the writer of Psalm 127:3 speaking about sons or is the writer speaking about daughters and sons?

It is true that the expression "the fruit of the womb" (Ps 127:3) can include both sons and daughters, but this expression occurs in parallel with the word *bānîm*, "sons," a word which occurs twice in the psalm (verses 3 and 4). In the Old Testament, when the writer wants to speak of sons and daughters, he will use words that include both genders (see Gen 5:4; 11:1; 19:12; 31:28; 36:6). For instance, when the writer wants to say Adam had many children, he wrote: "The days of Adam after he became the father of Seth were eight hundred years; and he had other sons and daughters" (Gen 5:4). The writer did not say, "Adam had other *bānîm*." Rather, he included both sons and daughters in his statement.

When the writer of Genesis wanted to say all the children of Jacob went into Egypt with him, he wrote that Jacob came with "his sons, and his sons' sons with him, his daughters, and his sons' daughters" (Gen 46:7). A better example appears in Exodus 21:4, where all three words, "sons," "daughters," and "children" appear together, each being represented by a different Hebrew word: "If his master gives him a wife and she bears him sons or daughters, the wife and her children shall be her master's and he shall go out alone" (Exod 21:4). The writer used *bānîm* for sons, *bānôt* for daughters, and *yeled* for children.

The people of Israel lived in a patriarchal society in which a family with many sons was considered to be a great blessing from God, while the absence of sons was considered as one of the severest punishments from God a family could receive.

This is the reason that Rachel, unable to conceive, cried to Jacob: "Give me sons, or I will die!" (Gen 30:1 HCSB). When Hannah, who was also unable to conceive, went to make a vow at the temple at Shiloh, her prayer was very specific: "Give to your servant a male child" (1 Sam 1:11 NRSV). In ancient Israel, the life of a father had meaning only insofar as it was continued in the life of his son. A son kept the name of the father from being forgotten in Israel. Absalom said: "I have no son to keep my name in remembrance"

(2 Sam 18:18). It is out of this cultural context that the psalmist declared sons were a blessing from the Lord. Many sons could help a father when he was old, primarily when he was engaged against his adversaries or when he was litigating at the city gate.

The psalmist said: "Unless the Lord builds the house, its builders labor in vain" (Ps 127:1). But once the house was built and the family had been established, then the man of the house had the responsibility of protecting his family. And it is out of this cultural context the reader must understand the words of the psalmist. Sons are divine blessings because they help their fathers bring protection and security to their family. A family with many sons was a theme that reflected the reality of Israel's culture. A large family with many sons was less vulnerable against hostile attacks. Thus, in a male-dominated society, sons were prized more than daughters.

The words of the psalmist reflect a warlike situation. Sons are "like arrows in the hand of a warrior." Sons are like a weapon. They are able to protect and defend their father when he is getting old and in need of support. A father who has many sons will not be put to shame before his enemies. A father would not be able to prevail against his enemies were it not for the support of his many sons. He who has many sons has his quiver full. Patrick D. Miller, in his book on the Psalms wrote: "The psalm seems to have in view primarily sons and the father rather than parents and children in general. The contemporary community can and should interpret the psalm in a more inclusive way, recognizing the joy and the reward for both mothers and fathers in having both sons and daughters."[1] However, when a contemporary community reads Psalm 127 and reads "children" rather than "sons," they find themselves separated from the cultural reality that gave birth to this psalm. Readers today, who live in a gender-inclusive society, will not appreciate the reality of ancient Israelite society that prized the value of sons for utilitarian reasons.

If the writer of Psalm 127 were to read his psalm in some versions today and find the word "children," he probably would say to the translator: "But this is not what I said." And the translator probably would say: "I know, but I am not translating for your culture, but for mine." And the despondent writer of Psalm 127 would say: "Yes, but this is not what I meant." The word "children" in Psalm 127:3 may reflect the reality of a twenty-first-century society that prizes inclusive language and the immense joy daughters bring to a family, but such a translation does not take seriously the historical realities of the culture that gave birth to this beautiful psalm.

1. Miller, *Interpreting the Psalms*, 134.

30

Proverbs 29:18

PROVERBS 29:18 IS ONE of the better known of the many proverbs in the book of Proverbs, but one that is the least understood and the one that is abused the most. Proverbs 29:18 has been used to defend political causes and to promote environmental issues. The primary reason for this misuse of Proverbs 29:18 is because of the translation of this verse as it appears in the KJV. The KJV translates Proverbs 29:18 as follows: "Where there is no vision, the people perish: but he that keepeth the law, happy is he." Now, compare the KJV with the translation that appears in the NRSV: "Where there is no prophecy, the people cast off restraint, but happy are those who keep the law." The reason for this difference is that the Hebrew word for vision, *ḥāzôn*, is generally used to designate the revelation of God's will to prophets. The word *ḥāzôn* is used to describe the visions of Isaiah (Isa 1:1) and of Nahum (Nah 1:1).

What the wiseman was trying to communicate to his audience was that without prophetic revelation and without the proclamation of the prophets calling the people into a faithful relationship with God and obedience to his word, people lose restraint and abandon God's law. The word of the wiseman reminded the people of the darkest time in the history of Israel when prophetic visions were not widespread: "In those days [the days of Samuel] the word of the LORD was rare and prophetic visions were not widespread" (1 Sam 3:1 HCSB). A few scholars have understood the lack of prophetic vision to mean that at the time this proverb was coined there were no prophets in Israel and the proclamation of the prophets was silent. However, this may not be necessarily the case.

Several times in the Bible it is said that divine revelation was withheld in times of Israel's apostasy. In the days when there was no king in Israel and people did whatever they wanted (Judg 21:25), the word of the LORD was rare and there was no frequent vision (1 Sam 3:1). The same sentiment was expressed by writers dealing with the consequences of the fall of Jerusalem: "Zion's gates have fallen to the ground; He has destroyed and shattered the bars on her gates. Her king and her leaders live among the nations, instruction is no more, and even her prophets receive no vision from the LORD" (Lam 2:9 HCSB). Ezekiel wrote: "Disaster after disaster will come, and there will be rumor after rumor. Then they will seek a vision from a prophet, but instruction will perish from the priests and counsel from the elders" (Ezek 7:26 HCSB).

The role of the prophets as interpreters of God's will to the people is reflected in the translation of Proverbs 29:18 in the Septuagint (LXX): "There shall be no interpreter to a sinful nation: but he that observes the law is blessed." When there is no one to teach, inspire, and exhort the people to be faithful to God, people perish. Without God's word to guide them, "people cast off restraint." This same Hebrew word was used twice to describe the people's depraved behavior during the celebration associated with the making of the golden calf: "Moses saw that the people were out of control, for Aaron had let them get out of control" (Exod 32:25).

The moral and spiritual problem of the community comes when prophecy ceases. The people cast off restraint when the voice of the prophets falls silent. When there is no one to bring a divine revelation to them, people will desperately seek God's word: "They shall wander from sea to sea, and from north to east; they shall run to and fro, seeking the word of the LORD, but they shall not find it" (Amos 8:12).

The wiseman said that people who willingly and earnestly submit themselves to the word of God are truly happy people. Law or Torah in Proverbs 29:18 means divine teaching, the word of God. The use of the word Torah ("law" or "teaching") in Proverbs 29:18 is not clear. It may be a reference to the Law of Moses, to the teachings of the prophets, or to the instructions of the wisemen. Whatever the meaning of the word Torah in Proverbs 29:18, Torah stands for God's word. Obedience to God's word is essential to the well-being of a nation or an individual: "Blessed is the nation whose God is the LORD, the people he chose for his inheritance" (Ps 33:12). People who hear and obey God's word enjoy a special blessing from God. However, they perish and are destroyed because they did not have knowledge of God's word: "My people are destroyed for lack of knowledge . . . [They] have forgotten the law of God" (Hos 4:6).

31

"Black and Beautiful" or "Black but Beautiful"?

SONG OF SONGS IS one of the most unfamiliar books of the Bible to many Christians because they do not read it very often. When they do, they wrongly call it "The Song of Solomon" believing Solomon wrote this beautiful song. In Hebrew, the title of the book is a superlative. The book should be translated "The Song of All Songs" or "The Greatest Song." Many Christians follow Jewish tradition and ascribe the authorship of the Song of Songs to Solomon. In fact, a Jewish tradition declares that when Solomon was young he wrote Proverbs, when he was in love he wrote Songs, and when he was old he wrote Ecclesiastes. None of these, of course, are true, but it serves to continue the idea that Solomon was the writer of these three biblical books.

As for the canonicity of Song of Songs, the book had some problems in being accepted as part of the canon. The reason for this reluctance is because Song of Songs tells a story of love with graphic sexual language. Most people reading Song of Songs in English will not notice the sexual language because the writer used euphemisms and metaphors to hide the sexuality of the dialogue between the woman and her lover. Eventually, the book was accepted as canonical because it was interpreted allegorically. Under this interpretation, Song of Songs describes the love of God for Israel or the love of Christ for the church. However, when properly understood, Song is a love story. The book describes in poetic form the love between a man and a woman.

Over the centuries, most readers of the book have struggled with the proper interpretation of this story of love. The traditional interpretation says the book tells the story of two lovers: Solomon and the Shulammite. For the proper interpretation of the story, it is important not to confuse the

Shulammite (Song 6:13) with Abishag the Shunammite of 1 Kings 1:3–4. They were two different persons.

Under the traditional interpretation of the Song, the book is telling the readers the story of Solomon's love for the Shulammite. The traditional interpretation also implies that Solomon wrote Song of Songs in order to express his love for the Shulammite. There is, however, a problem with the traditional interpretation. If the woman's lover was Solomon, then the reader must also assume Solomon was a shepherd who took care of his flock. For this reason, it is very clear Solomon was not the man the Shulammite loved.

A better interpretation of the Song sees three lovers in the story: Solomon, the Shulammite, and the one she loved, the shepherd.[1] Under this interpretation, Song is a story about Solomon and not a story by Solomon. This interpretation understands Song of Songs as a satire on Solomon. The story celebrates the victory of true love and tells of the occasion when Solomon's desire to have another woman as a member of his harem was foiled by a peasant woman who refused to exchange the man she loved for the comfort of the palace.

Here was a man who already had "sixty queens and eighty concubines, and maidens without number" (Song 6:8–9), but who wanted one more. But Solomon's display of riches and might (Song 3:6–11; 8:11) to gain the love of a peasant woman did not succeed. Solomon's wealth and royal position could not convince the woman to accept the king's advances and deny her love for the shepherd.

Song of Songs celebrates true love between a man and a woman, the kind of love that cannot be bought with money: "Many waters cannot quench love, neither can floods drown it. If a man offered for love all the wealth of his house, he would be utterly despised" (Song 8:7). Who was this remarkable woman, the Shulammite, who refused the wealth of Solomon and the enticement of royalty in order to remain true to her shepherd lover? The Bible has little to say about her. However, it is what she said about herself that has attracted the attention of many scholars. English translations differ on the interpretation of what the woman said about herself in Song 1:5. The NRSV translates her words as follows: "I am black and beautiful." The DRA translates as follows: "I am black but beautiful." The ESV translates as follows: "I am very dark, but lovely." The JPS translates as follows: "I am black, but comely." The Septuagint (LXX) translates as follows: "I am black, but beautiful."

---

1. Bullock, *Old Testament Poetical Books*, 217.

The Shulammite's words are addressed to the women of Jerusalem. Although the women do not respond, it is apparent that the women are looking at the Shulammite with disdain because of her appearance. She refers to her color and compares it with the tents of Kedar and the curtains of Solomon: "I am very dark, but comely, O daughters of Jerusalem, like the tents of Kedar, like the curtains of Solomon" (Song 1:5 RSV).

She said she had a dark complexion because she was exposed to the hot sun, since her brothers punished her by ordering her to take care of the vineyards: "Do not gaze at me because I am swarthy, because the sun has scorched me. My mother's sons were angry with me, they made me keeper of the vineyards; but, my own vineyard I have not kept" (Song 1:6 RSV). The text does not say her dark complexion was due to her racial background, that is, that she was an African woman. Her dark skin pigmentation was not a reference to a racial feature. What the Shulammite was trying to say to the women of Jerusalem was the exposure to the hot sun on her body made her darker than the women who lived in Jerusalem. She was dark because she did not protect her body from the intense heat of the sun.

The Shulammite's words reflect the fact that peasant women who worked in the fields had dark skin because of the constant exposure to the sun, while the women who lived in the luxurious houses of Jerusalem and those who lived in the palace were less dark than the peasant women who worked in the fields.

The woman explained her blackness by comparing it with the tents of Kedar and the curtains of Solomon. The tents of Kedar were Bedouin tents made of black goat hair. Although the text does not clarify what was intended by "the curtains of Solomon," they were probably curtains or wall hangings found in Solomon's palace known by its beauty and artistic designs. The reading of the HCSB tries to include both ideas in its translation, but in the process it diminishes what the Shulammite says about herself: "Daughters of Jerusalem, I am dark like the tents of Kedar, yet lovely like the curtains of Solomon."

The reason for the punishment her brothers inflicted on her was because she did not keep her own vineyard. The symbolism behind the vineyard is probably a reference to her virginity, that is, that she gave herself sexually to her shepherd lover and as a result her brothers punished her for her indiscretion. Thus, the Shulammite asked the women of Jerusalem not to pay attention to her black skin. In Hebrew the conjunction *waw* can be translated as "and" or "but." Many people object to translating the

Shulammite words as "black but beautiful" because such a translation may suggest blackness is not beautiful. Critics complain this translation may point to some kind of racial prejudice. A careful look at the text reveals the woman was explaining that although she had a dark complexion, she was beautiful. The reason she spoke about her dark skin was probably because it had become an issue in the minds of people who belonged to the upper class of Jerusalem. So the question must be asked: should the *waw* be translated as "and" or "but"?

A careful examination of the Shulammite words in light of her conversation with the women of Jerusalem reveals the woman was defending her dark skin. In addition, verse 6 explains her skin was dark because her brothers forced her to work in the vineyards and she was exposed to the hot sun. This is the reason she asks the women of Jerusalem not to look at her and her dark complexion with disdain. The text has nothing to do with race, neither is the text saying white skin is more attractive than dark skin. The problem is that today's society classifies people as back, white, or brown. Since this woman was a Semitic woman, she probably had dark skin. She was not white. The Shulammite defended her dark skin not because she believed it was ugly, but because her natural skin was not like that.

Thus, readers must conclude the woman was unhappy about her dark skin because it was not her natural skin color, but was the result of being exposed to the sun for a long time. The proper translation of 1:5 should be: "I am black but beautiful." However, when we read the words of the Shulammite, we can say with assurance, that she was black and beautiful, for the woman herself speaks unashamedly about her beauty, that she was black but beautiful.

SECTION FOUR

Prophetical Books

32

The Use of Gender-Inclusive Language

ONE DIFFICULT ISSUE IN Bible translation today is the use of gender-inclusive language. The debate is focused on whether the use of inclusive language changes the meaning of the text and misrepresents what the biblical author was trying to communicate. I am not against the use of inclusive language provided that the translation does not misrepresent the intent of the original text. Word-for-word translation is just not practical because one language does not precisely translate into another language. A translation of the Bible should be clear and accurate. It should communicate in English precisely what the biblical author was trying to communicate to the primary audience. At times, a good translation may require a little liberty with the text in order to communicate the real message of the original text, but the original intent of the writer must not be changed.

One verse where some translations have chosen to use inclusive language is Isaiah 9:1. (The versification is different in the Hebrew Bible. Isaiah 9:1 is 8:23 in the Hebrew Bible.) However, the use of inclusive language in Isaiah 9:1 has completely changed the original meaning of the text and fails to represent the intent of the message of the writer.

The proper understanding of Isaiah 9:1 requires a brief historical introduction. When Ahaz became king of Judah in 735 B.C.,[1] the nations of the ancient Near East were dealing with the menace posed by the Assyrian army and the policies of total conquest initiated by Tiglath-pileser III, king of Assyria, after he assumed the throne in 745 B.C. The Northern Kingdom was not immune to the threat posed by Assyria. When Pekahiah, the son

1. The dates for the kings of Judah and Israel follow the dates proposed by John Bright in his book *A History of Israel*.

of Menahem, became king in 738, he continued his father's policy of co-operation with Assyria. However, the burden of the tribute paid to Assyria convinced many Israelites it was time for change. In 737 B.C., Pekahiah was assassinated by Pekah, who was the third man in Pekahiah's war chariot. Pekah had the support of the anti-Assyrian faction in Israel and of those who advocated cooperation with Syria. Pekah came to the throne of Israel in order to foment revolt against Assyria. Pekah, king of Israel, and Rezin, king of Syria, formed an alliance in order to resist Tiglath-pileser. Acting in partnership, Pekah and Rezin turned their efforts to the south, to Judah, hoping to increase the size and strength of their armies.

At first, Jotham and then later, his son Ahaz, king of Judah refused to join the alliance. Rezin, king of Syria, and Pekah, king of Israel, invaded Judah in order to place on the throne Tabael (Isa 7:6), a man who would favor a joint alliance to fight against Assyria. This was the beginning of the Syro-Ephraimite War. Aware that his situation was precarious, and against the advice of the prophet Isaiah, Ahaz asked Tiglath-pileser for military help (2 Kgs 16:7). Ahaz paid a heavy tribute to Assyria. In order to gather the money needed for the tribute, Ahaz took gold and silver from the temple and from the royal treasury (2 Kgs 16:8). Ahaz sent messengers to Tiglath-pileser with the following message: "I am your servant and your son. Come up, and rescue me from the hand of the king of Syria and from the hand of the king of Israel, who are attacking me" (2 Kgs 16:7).

In response to Ahaz's invitation, Tiglath-pileser came to Palestine to help Judah. He conquered Philistia first and then invaded Syria. Tiglath-pileser "marched up against Damascus, and took it, carrying its people captive to Kir, and he killed Rezin" (2 Kgs 16:9). Then, Tiglath-pileser came against Israel, conquered several cities in Galilee and Naphtali and deported many people to Assyria: "In the time of Pekah king of Israel, Tiglath-Pileser king of Assyria came and took Ijon, Abel Beth Maacah, Janoah, Kedesh and Hazor. He took Gilead and Galilee, including all the land of Naphtali, and deported the people to Assyria" (2 Kgs 15:29).

A few years later, the prophet Isaiah proclaimed an oracle recorded in Isaiah 9:1–6 that is a direct reference to the events related to the Syro-Ephraimite War. Isaiah 9:1 has been translated differently by translators:

"But there will be no gloom for her who was in anguish" (Isa 9:1 ESV).

"But there will be no gloom for her that was in anguish" (Isa 9:1 RSV).

"But there will be no gloom for those who were in anguish" (Isa 9:1 NRSV).

"Nevertheless, there will be no more gloom for those who were in distress (Isa 9:1 NIV).

These four translations differ on how the first part of verse 1 is translated. The word "her" of the ESV and the RSV refers to the "land." The word "those" of the NIV and the NRSV refers to the people. The feminine pronoun in the Hebrew text requires the "her" be related to the land since the Hebrew word for land is also feminine. The ESV and the RSV say that because of the events related to the war, the land was in distress. The translation of the NIV and the NRSV distort the message of the verse and convey an incorrect impression to the reader by saying that because of the war, the people were in distress. The translation of the HCSB is direct and to the point: "Nevertheless, the gloom of the distressed land will not be like that of the former times" (Isa 9:1).

Why did the NIV and the NRSV choose to change the text and use "those" instead of "her" in translating the pronoun? There are two possible answers. First, the translators of the NIV and the NRSV understood the land ("her") to represent the people ("those"). However, this translation disregards the fact that the word "land" in "the land of Zebulun" and "the land of Naphtali" is feminine and is in direct relationship with the pronoun "her." Second, it is possible the translators were using gender-inclusive language and refused to use the word "her" in the same way they avoided using the word "him" in many places in their translation of the masculine pronoun.

I suspect the use of "those" in Isaiah 9:1 came out of a desire to be gender inclusive, but this effort at being gender inclusive completely changes the meaning of the text and does not allow the reader to grasp the real message of the prophet.

In their books, the prophets emphasize that the land suffers because of the sins of the people. Hosea said that because of the sins of the people, "the land mourns" (Hos 4:3). Because of the sins of the people, the land was defiled and became an abomination (Jer 2:7). The message of Isaiah must be understood in the context of the Syro-Ephraimite War: because of the sins of the people, the land was in distress.

The translation of the NIV and the NRSV is unfortunate. Those who read Isaiah 9:1 in these translations may have compassion for the people who were in distress, but they will feel nothing for the land, the real concern of the prophet. And the only reason the reader will be unable to sympathize with the distress of the land is because somewhere a committee decided to be politically correct rather than convey the real message of the prophet.

33

"You Have Increased Their Joy"

A FEW STUDENTS OF the Bible have noticed the reading of Isaiah 9:3 (H 9:2) in the KJV differs from the reading in other versions of the Bible. The purpose of this study is to explain why the KJV differs from other English translations. Below are two translations of Isaiah 9:3:

> KJV: "Thou hast multiplied the nation, *and not increased the joy*: they joy before thee according to the joy in harvest, and as men rejoice when they divide the spoil."

> JPS: "Thou hast multiplied the nation, *Thou hast increased their joy*; they joy before Thee according to the joy in harvest, as men rejoice when they divide the spoil."

I have emphasized the section of verse 3 where the versions differ. As can be seen above, one version (the KJV) is negative, "*and not increased the joy*," while the other version (the JPS) is positive, "*Thou hast increased their joy*." The question is: why the difference? The answer to this question and the explanation as to why the two versions differ in their translation of the text is found in the Hebrew Bible and in the notes provided by the Masoretes.

The Masoretes were Jewish scribes who copied the ancient Hebrew manuscripts. They added the vowels to the consonantal text, marked doubtful passages, and divided the text into sections for liturgical use. One of the greatest contributions of the Masoretes was the marginal notes they added to the manuscripts. These notes provided alternative readings of the texts they believed represented a more correct reading than those found in the manuscripts. These notes are called the *ketiv/qere*. The *ketiv*, "that which is written," is the form of the word that appears in the Hebrew Bible. The *qere*, "that which is to be read," is the correction made by the scribes, which in their opinion represents an ancient and better reading.

One of those proposed emendations is found in Isaiah 9:3 and the issue here is a homophone. Homophones are words that when read are pronounced alike but have different meaning or are spelled differently. One good example of homophones in English is found in the words "to," "too," and "two." The homophone in Hebrew is לֹא and לוֹ. The two words sound alike when they are pronounced in Hebrew, but they have different meanings. The first word לֹא, *lō'*, means "not," and the second word לוֹ, *lô*, means "to him," "his." The Hebrew text of Isaiah 9:3 reads as follows: הִגְדַּלְתָּ הַשִּׂמְחָה לֹא (*lō' higdaltā hassimhāh*).

The King James translates the text as: *Thou hast not increased the joy*. This is the *ketiv* or what is written in the text. However, the Masoretes said this is not the best and original reading. Thus, they put a note in the margin of the text and said that instead of reading לֹא (*lō'*), "not," the text should read לוֹ (*lô*, "to him"). *"Thou hast increased their joy,"* or "you have increased joy to him." This is the *qere*, what should be read.

Now, when it came time to translate Isaiah 9:3 into English, of all the modern versions, only the KJV adopted the *ketiv* reading, the reading of the Hebrew text. All the other versions, including the NKJV followed the *qere*, or the reading proposed by the Masoretes. A closer look at the context of the passage demonstrates that "Thou hast increased their joy" is the better reading. According to the text, the Lord enlarged the nation and increased their joy. In addition, the people rejoiced before the Lord in the same way they rejoiced at harvest time and when they divided spoils.

It is unfortunate the KJV did not follow the *qere* in translating Isaiah 9:3 since the negative translation adopted by the KJV contradicts the message the prophet was trying to convey to his audience. The mood of joy and celebration that would be demonstrated by the people affirms that the *qere* reading, *"Thou hast increased their joy,"* is the correct reading of Isaiah 9:3.

34

Who Will the Messiah Strike?

SOME ENGLISH VERSIONS DIFFER on how to translate and interpret a section of Isaiah 11:4. The three translations quoted below reflect the problem translators face in translating and interpreting Isaiah 11:4. The NRSV translates Isaiah 11:4 as follows: "He shall strike the earth with the rod of his mouth." The BBE translates Isaiah 11:4 as follows: "And the rod of his mouth will come down on the cruel." The NAB translates Isaiah 11:4 as follows: "He shall strike the ruthless with the rod of his mouth."

The reason for this difference among the translations cited above is because the word אֶרֶץ ('reṣ, "earth") is taken by some scholars to be an error for עָרִיץ ('ārîṣ, "ruthless"). The Qumran scroll of Isaiah reads אֶרֶץ ('reṣ, "earth") and the Septuagint reads γῆς (gēs, "land"). The reason some translations propose this correction is because the word 'reṣ ("earth") appears in parallelism with רָשָׁע (rāshā', "wicked") in Isaiah 11:4: "and he shall smite the earth with the rod of his mouth; and with the breath of his lips shall he slay the wicked." Thus, according to some scholars, the best parallel for the word "wicked" is the word "ruthless." This correction has been suggested by *Biblia Hebraica* (BHK) and by *Biblia Hebraica Sttugartentia* (BHS) and it has been accepted by some scholars.

For instance, Otto Kaiser in his commentary on Isaiah said that, in order to implement his verdict against the oppressor of the poor, one word from the king's mouth "is enough to kill the evildoer."[1] H. G. Mitchell, in his commentary on Isaiah writes: "The text has אֶרֶץ, 'the land,' which does not express the evident thought of the author. It is expressed by the word

1. Kaiser, *Isaiah 1–12*, 258.

עָרִיץ, 'the violent,' which, moreover, occurs several times as a synonym of the term godless (see Jer. xv. 21). It is safe, therefore, to conclude, that this was the original reading."[2] T. K. Cheyne, in his book, *The Prophecies of Isaiah*, says: "The received reading gives the passage a different and rather less appropriate term. The 'earth' must be the hostile, heathen world, and the 'ungodly' a collective term for its rulers (comp. Ps. cxxv. 3, 'the sceptre of ungodliness'), and the prophet will then allude to the judicial act of vengeance which, down to the time of John the Baptist, was regarded as chronologically the first function of the Messiah."[3]

However, even though the word "ruthless" would make a better parallelism to the word "wicked," it is difficult to accept this proposed emendation when all the textual evidence seems to confirm the original reading. The prophet is saying that in establishing justice on the earth, the righteous king will apply a just and impartial use of power in the defense of the weak against the earthly powers that oppress the poor and the defenseless.

2. Mitchell, *Isaiah*, 245.

3. Cheyne, *The Prophecies of Isaiah*, 76.

35

The Way of the Lord

When Deutero-Isaiah wrote about "the way of the Lord" being made straight (Isa 40:3), the prophet was declaring that, when the people of Israel left Babylon, the Lord would not allow his people to stumble. When God directs the way of an individual, that person has all the help needed not to fall down or stumble. The translation of the word "way" (Hebrew *derek*) takes different meanings in the Old Testament. The word *derek* can be translated to mean a road, journey, manner, and custom.[1] The word *derek* is also used as a metaphor for the actions and behavior of human beings as in Psalm 1. Used as a figurative language, the word *derek* also means the way people live their lives. Several passages in the Old Testament, such as Proverbs 3:6; 11:5; 3:23; and Isaiah 40:3 show that when the Lord guides the way of an individual, that person will not "fall down or stumble."

Proverbs 3:6 says: "In all your ways acknowledge him, and he will make straight your paths" (ESV). In this passage, the word "ways" includes all the acts and actions of a person; these acts can be both spiritual and secular. Thus, the psalmist is urging people to recognize God in all their endeavors, to pray for divine guidance, and to ask God's direction in every aspect of life.

Proverbs 11:5 says: "The righteousness of the blameless keeps his way straight, but the wicked falls by his own wickedness" (ESV). The word "way" in this passage conveys the same ideas found in Proverbs 3:6. The righteousness of righteous individuals determines their lives, but the ungodliness of evil people will cause them to fall.

1. BDB, 202.

Proverbs 3:23 says: "Then you will walk on your way securely, and your foot will not stumble" (ESV). The wise are teaching that those who do not abandon wisdom and put into practice the counsel of the wise will live life in such a way that their wisdom will help them walk in their way securely and their feet will not stumble. In short, they shall enjoy the greatest sense of security in all situations of their lives.

Isaiah 40:3 says: "A voice cries: 'In the wilderness prepare the way of the Lord; make straight in the desert a highway for our God'" (ESV). In this verse, the word "way" does not have the same meaning as the verses in Proverbs. Here it is clear that the text is not talking about the way people live their lives. In order to understand the meaning of the word "way" in the preaching of the exilic prophet, it is important to understand his historical context.

At the time the prophet hears these words, the people of Israel are in exile in Babylon. The Lord has come to announce to Israel that her exile, "her time of service," has been completed and the time for her deliverance has dawned (Isa 40:2). The Lord is calling his people to prepare to return home and now has come to assure them that all the difficulties standing in the way of their deliverance shall be removed. The unknown voice is declaring that the Lord is preparing to conduct his people back to their own country through the wilderness, in the same way he had long ago led them from Egypt to Canaan. The prophet hears the voice of a herald instructing that a way should be made in the wilderness for the return home of the people (Isa 40:3).

The whole scene is represented as a triumphal march of a king. Yahweh is at the head of his people to lead them back home. As Claus Westermann, in his commentary on *Isaiah 40–66* has shown, this idea is taken from the practice of kings in the ancient Near East. Before kings traveled, they sent heralds before them to prepare the way through the desert. At the command of the king, his servants leveled hills, constructed causeways over valleys, or filled them up to make a straight highway for the royal entourage. Westermann writes:

> Triumphal highways, ways prepared and made level for the triumphal entry of the god or king, were also well-known in Babylon.
> . . . They are the background . . . of the present passage . . . these imposing highways were symbols of Babylon's might, the might that had brought about Israel's own downfall." These are the circumstances in which they heard the cry to make straight in the desert a highway, a highway 'for Yahweh . . . our God'. . . . [T]he highway of which the prophet thinks is the one that is to enable Israel to make her way homeward through the desert. It is, however,

> designated a highway 'for our God', just as the magnificent high-
> ways of Babylon were strictly highways for her god.[2]

Thus, God's herald says: "In the wilderness prepare the way of the Lord; make straight in the desert a highway for our God. Every valley shall be lifted up, and every mountain and hill be made low; the uneven ground shall become level, and the rough places a plain" (Isa 40:3–4 ESV). What the Lord wanted was a leveled road, an *autobahn* in the desert so the people could reach their destination without delay. The same declaration of the unknown voice reappears in the New Testament, but the New Testament writers do not follow the Hebrew text; they follow the translation found in the Septuagint.

The Septuagint, the Greek translation of the Old Testament, mistranslated this verse. The translators, instead of placing the accent, which causes a pause, after the verb "cries," placed it after the word "wilderness." Thus, instead of translating: "A voice cries: 'In the wilderness prepare the way of the Lord'" (Isa 40:3), the Septuagint translates: "The voice of one crying in the wilderness: 'Prepare ye the way of the Lord.'" This is the translation adopted by the KJV. This same translation was also adopted in the New Testament by the writers of the Gospels. For instance, Matthew 3:3 says: "For this is he who was spoken of by the prophet Isaiah when he said, 'The voice of one crying in the wilderness: Prepare the way of the Lord; make his paths straight'" (ESV). However, the Hebrew accent and the parallelism of the verse demand a separation between "cries" and "wilderness." The parallelism of the verse in Isaiah 40:3 looks as follows:

> In the wilderness prepare the way of the Lord,
> make straight in the desert a highway for our God.
> Every valley shall be lifted up, and every mountain and hill be
> made low;
> the uneven ground shall become level, and the rough places a plain.

In the apocryphal book of Baruch, the words of the exilic prophet are taken as a call for the people to return home. The text reads: "Arise, O Jerusalem, stand upon the height; look toward the east, and see your children gathered from west and east at the word of the Holy One, rejoicing that God has remembered them. For they went out from you on foot, led away by their enemies; but God will bring them back to you, carried in glory, as on a royal throne. For God has ordered that every high mountain and the everlasting

---

2. Westermann, *Isaiah 40–66*, 38.

hills be made low and the valleys filled up, to make level ground, so that Israel may walk safely in the glory of God" (Bar 5:5–7).

So, it is true, the way of the Lord is made straight, but it is made straight for the sake of his people.

36

"All Their Goodliness"

ALTHOUGH THE BIBLE IS the most beloved and the most read book in the world, it is probably also the most misunderstood. One of the reasons for this is many people read the Bible, but never take time to study it in detail. People who love the Bible read those holy words for knowledge, edification, and spiritual nourishment. They may read the words of the Old Testament over and over again and find joy and peace for their souls and answers for the problems of life, and yet they may miss the precise meaning of what the original author intended to communicate to his audience. The average readers of the Old Testament may be familiar with its content and words. They may read one verse or one chapter and meditate on what was read and discover what the Bible says about God, the human predicament, and how to discover comfort in the midst of suffering, and yet, without fully grasping the message the writer was addressing to his audience.

Take for instance this reading from the KJV: "The voice said, cry. And he said, 'What shall I cry?' All flesh is grass, and all the goodliness thereof is as the flower of the field" (Isa 40:6). In order to discover whether people understood the message of this verse, several church members were asked to read this verse twice and then define the word "goodliness." Most people who read the passage believed the word "goodliness" had something to do with the goodness of people. This is how the HCSB understands the verse: "A voice was saying, 'Cry out!' 'What should I cry out?' All humanity is grass, and all its goodness is like the flower of the field." However, in the context of Isaiah 40, the word "goodliness" is used in the sense of elegance, comeliness, or beauty.

One commentator understood the word to be an attempt to make a contrast between people (all flesh) and grass. He said the prophet's intent was to emphasize that all people are weak and feeble like the grass that is soon withered. To him, this comparison refers to all people, in all places, and at all times. This passage in Isaiah is quoted in 1 Peter 1:24: "All flesh is as grass, and all the glory of man as the flower of grass" (KJV). Several modern translations are influenced by the text of 1 Peter and follow the example of the KJV.

The NIV 1984 translates Isaiah 40:6 as follows: "A voice says, 'cry out.' And I said, 'What shall I cry?' All men are like grass, and all their glory is like the flowers of the field." The RSV translates: "A voice says, 'cry!' And I said, 'What shall I cry?' All flesh is grass, and all its beauty is like the flower of the field." The NJB translates: "A voice said, 'cry aloud!' and I said, 'What shall I cry?' All humanity is grass and all its beauty like the wild flowers."

All the translations cited above are influenced by the Septuagint, the Greek translation of the Old Testament, which came into existence in the second century before the Christian era. The Septuagint translates the Hebrew word *hesed* as *doxa* and so does 1 Peter (1 Pet 1:24). The word *doxa* means "glory."

Explaining how the word *doxa* is used in Isaiah 40:6, Albert Barnes writes in his commentary:

> Applied to grass, or to herbs, it denotes the flower, the beauty, the comeliness. Applied to man, it means that which makes him comely and vigorous—health, energy, beauty, talent, and wisdom. His vigor is soon gone; his beauty fades; his wisdom ceases; and he falls, like the flower, to the dust. The idea is, that the plans of man must be temporary; that all that appears great in him must be like the flower of the field; but that Yahweh endures, and his plans reach from age to age, and will certainly be accomplished. This important truth was to be proclaimed, that the people might be induced not to trust in man, but put their confidence in the arm of God.[1]

The word that appears in the Hebrew text of Isaiah and is translated "goodliness" in the KJV is *hesed*. The word *hesed* is related to the covenant God established with Israel at Sinai. The word *hesed* refers to the commitment that binds two parties to a relationship.

In his book, *The Word Hesed in the Hebrew Bible*, Gordon Clark says *hesed* is an "action performed, in the context of a deep and enduring

---

1. Barnes, *Isaiah*, 2:59.

commitment between two persons or parties."[2] Since faithfulness to a relationship is a character of God, God also expects his people to be as committed to the relationship as he is.

When the word is applied to God, it refers to his faithfulness to the relationship. Thus, the word is best translated as "faithfulness," "unfailing love," "loyalty." When the word is applied to human beings it refers to the loyalty and commitment people should bring to that relationship. In this case, a good translation of *hesed* should be "commitment," "loyalty." A strong relationship is built on commitment. Israel should be as loyal and committed to the covenant as God was.

The NRSV has a much better translation of this verse: "A voice says, 'cry out!' And I said, 'What shall I cry?' All people are grass, their constancy is like the flower of the field" (Isa 40:6). The TNIV also reflects the intent of the writer: "A voice says: 'cry out.' And I said, 'What shall I cry?' All people are like grass, and all human faithfulness is like the flower of the field." The NIV 2011 also has a better translation: "A voice says, 'cry out.' And I said, 'What shall I cry?' All people are like grass, and all their faithfulness is like the flowers of the field."

God promised to be faithful to his relationship with Israel and he was. The people of Israel promised to be faithful to their covenant with God, but they were not. Thus, what the prophet was trying to communicate was the people's commitment was like the flower of the field, which is here today and gone tomorrow. This was the same idea expressed by the prophet Hosea: "What shall I do with you, O Ephraim? What shall I do with you, O Judah? Your love (*hesed*) is like a morning cloud, like the dew that goes away early" (Hos 6:4 NRSV).

In Isaiah 40:6 the prophet was saying the commitment of Israel to the covenant was like the flower of the field: it did not last very long. He was also saying that God's word, his promises to Israel, endures forever because God is faithful to his commitment to Israel. We must reread Isaiah 40:6 from a different perspective and learn anew that God does not want "goodliness." God wants the commitment of his people.

2. Clark, *The Word Hesed*, 267.

37

The Proclaimer of Good News

IN THE CHAPTERS ON Hosea and Amos I will point out inconsistencies in the way the NIV translates some Hebrew words. These inconsistencies are not helpful to pastors who preach and teach from the NIV. They are also not helpful to lay people who use only one version of the Bible and do not use other versions to compare translations of specific verses. In this chapter I want to sing the praises of the NIV. I do not do this very often because in many places, the translation of the NIV does not reflect the intent of the original writers of the biblical text. One place where I believe the NIV is superior to the NRSV, the KJV, and the ESV is in Isaiah 40:9. In these three translations, Isaiah 40:9 reads as follows:

> NRSV: "Get you up to a high mountain, O Zion, herald of good tidings; lift up your voice with strength, O Jerusalem, herald of good tidings, lift it up, do not fear; say to the cities of Judah, 'Here is your God!'"

> KJV: "O Zion, that bringest good tidings, get thee up into the high mountain; O Jerusalem, that bringest good tidings, lift up thy voice with strength; lift it up, be not afraid; say unto the cities of Judah, Behold your God!"

> ESV: "Get you up to a high mountain, O Zion, herald of good news; lift up your voice with strength, O Jerusalem, herald of good news; lift it up, fear not; say to the cities of Judah, 'Behold your God!'"

The NIV translates Isaiah 40:9 as follows: "You who bring good tidings to Zion, go up on a high mountain. You who bring good tidings to

Jerusalem, lift up your voice with a shout, lift it up, do not be afraid; say to the towns of Judah, 'Here is your God!'"

In the NRSV, the KJV, and the ESV it is Zion (Jerusalem) who is commanded to go to a high mountain, and it is Zion (Jerusalem), who, as the herald of good news, is commanded to proclaim to the cities of Judah the advent of Yahweh. These three translations differentiate between the messenger who proclaims good news on God's behalf in verse 6 and Zion as the messenger who proclaims good news to the cities of Judah. The form of the Hebrew word מְבַשֶּׂרֶת (mebassereth) is not difficult to understand. It literally means: "one who bears good tidings". The Greek Septuagint translates: "the one bringing good news to Zion". The Latin Vulgate translates: "you who evangelizes Zion".

The verb mebassereth is a participle feminine. In Hebrew, the participle feminine form of the verb is used to denote an office or an occupation such as sōphereth, the office of the sōpher or scribe (Ezra 2:55; Neh 7:5). Thus, the mebassereth in Isaiah 40:9 is a title that should be applied to someone who was appointed to proclaim good news to Zion. The title should not be applied to Zion as the one appointed to proclaim good news to the cities of Judah. Thus, I believe the NIV translation, which regards Zion as the receiver, and not the proclaimer of the good news, is a better translation.

The text in Isaiah is not calling upon Jerusalem to make known the good news to the cities of Judah. Rather, the messenger of God is to proclaim the good news to Jerusalem; he is to announce to Jerusalem (and in a sense, to the people of Judah), that after many years of lying desolate and waste, her time of servitude has come to an end and that the time of release would soon come to pass (Isa 40:2).

The translation found in the NRSV, the KJV, and the ESV is awkward, because it gives Jerusalem the duty to proclaim to the other cities of Judah that the exile was over for the nation. It is also awkward to believe that the city of Jerusalem was called to go up into a high mountain and proclaim to the other cities of Judah that the Lord was about to bring the people back to the land.

Thus, when it comes to Isaiah 40:9, I have to sing the praises of the NIV. And this commendation of the NIV has something important to say about Bible translations. Every translation of the Bible has its strengths and weaknesses. No translation of the Bible is perfect, not even the King James Version. Serious students of the Bible must learn how to use more than one version of the Bible and compare translations to gain a better perspective of the intent of the original writer. When translations differ, and they will differ, Bible students must consult good exegetical commentaries to gain a better perspective of what the biblical writers were trying to communicate to their readers and to us.

38

The Problem of Divorce in the Old Testament

WHEN THE HOLMAN CHRISTIAN Standard Bible (HCSB) was published, one reviewer disagreed with its translation of Isaiah 50:1. The HCSB translates Isaiah 50:1 as follows: "This is what the LORD says: 'Where is your mother's divorce certificate that I used to send her away? Or who were My creditors that I sold you to? Look, you were sold for your iniquities, and your mother was put away because of your transgressions.'" The reviewer proposed that the expression "send her away" should be translated as "get rid of her" or probably "divorce her." In this chapter I will defend the translation proposed by the HCSB. I believe the criticism of the HCSB's translation does not do justice to the complicated problem of divorce in the Old Testament.

First, it is important to notice that all translations, ancient and modern, support the HCSB's translation. For instance, this is the translation of Isaiah 50:1 in the ESV, NIV, and the RSV:

> ESV: "Thus says the LORD: 'Where is your mother's certificate of divorce, with which I sent her away?'"

> NIV: "This is what the LORD says: 'Where is your mother's certificate of divorce with which I sent her away?'"

> RSV: "Thus says the LORD: 'Where is your mother's bill of divorce, with which I put her away?'"

Even the Septuagint agrees with the classical translation of this verse: "Thus saith the Lord, 'Of what kind is your mother's bill of divorcement, by which I put her away?'" Second, in order to understand the reason these translations are right and the proposed correction is unacceptable, one must look at the issue of divorce in the Old Testament. In the Old Testament it was the husband who ended a marriage since the woman did not have the right to separate herself from her husband. When a man wanted to terminate an unacceptable marriage, he would simply send his wife away. Since a woman was considered the possession of her husband, she could not marry again because she was still legally married to her husband. A divorced woman was destitute and without the legal protection of her husband. Often, a divorced woman was also refused readmission into her family because the bridal price paid by the husband caused the woman to be legally under the control of her husband. Without the support of her husband or her family, divorced women were forced to beg and to become prostitutes in order to survive. In order to deal with this problem, the Deuteronomic reform under Josiah enacted a law to protect divorced women. The law reads:

> When a man takes a wife and marries her, if then she finds no favor in his eyes because he has found some indecency in her, and he writes her a certificate of divorce and puts it in her hand and sends her out of his house, and she departs out of his house, and if she goes and becomes another man's wife, and the latter man hates her and writes her a certificate of divorce and puts it in her hand and sends her out of his house, or if the latter man dies, who took her to be his wife, then her former husband, who sent her away, may not take her again to be his wife, after she has been defiled, for that is an abomination before the LORD (Deut 24:1–4 ESV).

This Deuteronomic law gives a man the right to put his wife away, but whenever he sends her away, he must provide her with a certificate of divorce. The certificate of divorce allows a divorced woman to remarry if she so desires.

The issues of divorce and sending away appear in the New Testament. In Matthew 19:3 a Pharisee asked Jesus: "Is it lawful to divorce one's wife for any cause?" Jesus' answer did not please the Pharisee. So he asked another question: "Why then did Moses command one to give a certificate of divorce and to send her away?" (Matt 19:7).

The issue raised in Deuteronomy 24:1–4 and in Matthew 19:1–8 is based on the fact that when a man sends his wife away (and this is not figurative language), he is not divorcing her, he is merely sending her away without any legal protection. When a man sends a woman away, the woman is still married to her husband. This is the reason she cannot belong to another man: she is still married. The Hebrew makes a difference between sending a woman away and divorcing her. In Hebrew, the word שָׁלַח

(shālaḥ) means "to send away" while the word כְּרִיתֻת (kĕrîthûth) means to dissolve the marriage by giving the woman a certificate of divorce.

The word shālaḥ appears in Malachi 2:16. However, translators are divided on how to translate the word. These are some of the versions that translate shālaḥ as "putting away" or "sending away": LXX, ASV, KJV, and JPS. These are some of the versions that translate shālaḥ as "divorce": ESV, NIV, RSV, and NRSV. The reason Yahweh hates "sending away" is because sending away is an illegal separation: the woman was put out of the house of her husband without a certificate of divorce.

In addition to Deuteronomy 24:1, the words shālaḥ and kĕrîthûth appear together in Jeremiah 3:8: "She saw that for all the adulteries of that faithless one, Israel, I had sent her away with a decree of divorce" (Jer 3:8 ESV). The two words also appear together in Isaiah 50:1: "Thus says the LORD: Where is your mother's certificate of divorce, with which I sent her away?" (Isa 50:1 ESV).

It is clear then that in the Old Testament "sending away" does not necessarily mean "divorce." It means a man "gets rid of" his wife and sends her away from his house without any legal protection. Thus, the proposed revision, "get rid of her" or "divorce her" would not be correct in the context of Isaiah 50:1 because the two proposed suggestions do not reflect the practice of divorce in the Old Testament. The expression "get rid of her" could be used in Malachi 2:16 because the sending away was an illegal separation, but not in Isaiah 50:1 because the woman was legally divorced.

The expression "divorce her" could not be used in Malachi 2:16 because the separation was illegal. The same expression also cannot be used in Isaiah 50:1 because once the woman was legally divorced (this is the intent of the certificate of divorce) the woman was sent away from her former husband's house. The reviewer's proposal, "Where is your mother's divorce certificate that I used to divorce her?" may not indicate that she was sent away from her husband's house. I support the HCSB's translation.

39

Beulah Land

A HYMN THAT WAS a favorite of Christians a generation ago was "Beulah Land," a hymn written by Edgar Page Stites and John R. Sweney:

I've reached the land of corn and wine,
And all its riches freely mine;
Here shines undimmed one blissful day,
For all my night has passed away.
Refrain
O Beulah Land, sweet Beulah Land,
As on thy highest mount I stand,
I look away across the sea,
Where mansions are prepared for me,
And view the shining glory shore,
My Heav'n, my home forever more!
My Savior comes and walks with me,
And sweet communion here have we;
He gently leads me by His hand,
For this is Heaven's border land.[1]

The beauty of this hymn is that it speaks of the eternal glory prepared for believers. Beulah Land is "Heaven's border land," a land where "shines undimmed one blissful day, for all my night has passed away." Today, this beautiful hymn is seldom sung in churches where praise songs and contemporary Christian rock music dominate the worship experience. But this phenomenon

1. Edgar P. Stites and John R. Sweney, "Beulah Land," public domain.

is not peculiar to contemporary churches. A brief survey of hymnals from several denominations reveals that this hymn is either unknown or no longer relevant to many churches. The theme of Beulah Land appears in many Christian hymns, but many people who know the hymn, sing its words, and love its message do not know the story behind Beulah Land.

The concept of Beulah Land comes from a passage found in Isaiah 62:4. The reason many people are unfamiliar with the concept of Beulah Land is because the word appears only in older translations of Isaiah 62:4, including the King James Version and the American Standard Version of 1901: "Thou shalt no more be termed Forsaken; neither shall thy land any more be termed Desolate: but thou shalt be called Hephzibah, and thy land Beulah; for Jehovah delighteth in thee, and thy land shall be married" (Isa 62:4 ASV).

The words of the prophet are words of encouragement: "You shall no more be termed Forsaken" (Isa 62:4 ESV). Because of its exile in Babylon, the people of Judah believed God had forsaken his people: "Zion said, 'The LORD has forsaken me, my Lord has forgotten me'" (Isa 49:14). The people's feelings were not completely without merit, for the Lord himself had affirmed that for a short moment he had actually forsaken them: "I did forsake you for a brief moment" (Isa 54:7). Even Israel's enemies, in derision, mocked the people by calling their land "Desolate."

After the Babylonian invasion under Nebuchadnezzar, the land became waste and desolate, a land of ruins (Isa 49:19). The cities of Judah had become a "desolation" (Jer 34:22).

But now, with the redemption of Israel and the return of the people to their land, things changed. The land that once was desolate has become like the garden of Eden; and the waste, desolate, and ruined cities are now fortified and inhabited, just as the prophet Ezekiel had proclaimed (Ezek 36:35). From now on, with the restoration of Israel, the land will be called "Hephzibah." This word literally means "My Delight Is in Her." The land also will be Beulah. The word "Beulah" means "married." The metaphor of marriage is used in the Old Testament to describe the relationship between God and his people. The concept of Yahweh as Israel's husband appears in Hosea, Jeremiah, and Ezekiel. This idea is clearly expressed in Isaiah 62:5: "As the bridegroom rejoices over the bride, so shall your God rejoice over you."

All the modern translations, contrary to the KJV and a few other old translations, translate the word "Beulah," rather than allow the word to remain untranslated. For instance, the ESV correctly translates Isaiah 62:4 as follows: "You shall no more be termed Forsaken, and your land shall no more be termed Desolate, but you shall be called My Delight Is in Her, and your land Married; for the LORD delights in you, and your land shall be married."

The correct interpretation of Isaiah 62:4 clearly shows that Beulah Land carries no idea of "Heaven's border land," a land where "shines undimmed one blissful day," where all our nights have passed away. If this idea is a central message of the hymn, from where then, does the idea of Beulah Land as heaven's border land come?

To the surprise of many, the idea of the land of Beulah as heaven's border land comes from John Bunyan's *Pilgrim Progress.* In his work, Bunyan says "the Enchanted Ground was a place near the land Beulah and so near the end of pilgrims race."[2] He also says the land of Beulah is the place "where the sun shineth night and day."[3]

Bunyan's concept of Beulah land as heaven's border land entered into Christian hymns through the Holiness Movement in America.[4] In his writings, Stites writes the following words about Beulah Land:

> It was in 1876 that I wrote "Beulah Land." I could write only two verses and the chorus, when I was overcome and fell on my face. That was one Sunday. On the following Sunday I wrote the third and fourth verses, and again I was so influenced by emotion that I could only pray and weep. The first time it was sung was at the regular Monday morning meeting of Methodists in Philadelphia [Pennsylvania]. Bishop McCabe sang it to the assembled ministers. Since then it is known wherever religious people congregate. I have never received a cent for my songs. Perhaps that is why they have had such a wide popularity. I could not do work for the Master and receive pay for it."[5]

2. Bunyan, *Pilgrim's Progress*, 252.

3. Ibid., 464.

4. My former student, Karen Roberts, wrote a research paper for one of my courses in which she traced the development of Beulah Land in Christian hymnody and the Holiness Movement in America. Roberts listed 13 different hymns that use the Beulah Land metaphor.

5. Edgar P. Stites, "Beulah Land," http://www.hymntime.com/tch/htm/b/e/u/beulah2.htm (accessed July 21, 2012).

40

The Balm of Gilead

"Is THERE NO BALM in Gilead? Is there no physician there? Why then is there no healing for the wound of my people?" (Jer 8:22 NIV). This verse in the book of the prophet Jeremiah is well known to readers of the Bible. It has been popularized in scores of titles of books, sermons, and in a well-known African-American spiritual hymn, "There Is a Balm in Gilead":

> There is a balm in Gilead
> To make the wounded whole;
> There is a balm in Gilead
> To heal the sin sicksoul.

This hymn interprets Jeremiah's words Christologically because the words of the hymn assume Christ is the Balm of Gilead that can "heal the sin sicksoul." Although the text is well known, many of the interpretations of the words of the prophet do not reflect the true intent of Jeremiah's message to the people of Judah. For instance, in a book titled *The Wonderful Names of Our Wonderful Lord*, T. C. Horton and Charles E. Hurlburt called Jesus "The Balm of Gilead."[1] This, however, is not what Jeremiah meant when he spoke about the balm of Gilead.

Another problem scholars have with this text is giving the right answer to Jeremiah's question. Is the answer to Jeremiah's question "No, there is no balm in Gilead and no, there are no physicians there." Or is the answer "Yes, there is balm in Gilead and yes, there are physicians there." C. F. Keil, in his commentary on Jeremiah, writes: "To these questions a negative answer is

1. Horton and Hurlburt, *The Wonderful Names*, 55.

given: if there were balm in Gilead and a physician there, then a plaister would have been laid on the daughter of my people, which is not the case."[2]

In his discussion of Jeremiah's words, Fleming Rutledge writes: "When Jeremiah spoke those words, he had every reason to believe that the answer was *no*. If we don't understand that there really might not have been any, we will never understand the magnitude of God's saving work."[3] Terence Fretheim believes the answer is positive. He writes: "The first two questions are rhetorical: Yes, there is balm in Gilead; yes, there are physicians there; but, it is implied, they are powerless to restore health to a patient with this kind of illness."[4] Peter C. Craigie, Page H. Kelley, and Joel F. Drinkard Jr., in their commentary on Jeremiah, take an ambivalent position. They write: "The natural answer to these questions would have to be yes but the reality of the situation demands that Jeremiah answer no."[5]

The purpose of this chapter is to provide an alternative reading to Jeremiah's words, a reading that, I believe, reflects the true intent of what Jeremiah was trying to communicate to his audience.

The balm of Gilead was an ointment made from the resin of a tree that was used as a healing ointment. The identity of this tree is unknown although many solutions have been proposed. According to the Old Testament, the balm of Gilead was used for medicine, perfume, and body ointment. According to Genesis 37:25, an Ishmaelite caravan traveled from Gilead carrying spices, balm, and myrrh to sell their merchandise in Egypt. Jeremiah tells the Egyptians to go to Gilead and use its balm because they had used many medicines without finding healing for their sickness (Jer 46:11).

Before a proper identification of the balm of Gilead and of the physicians can be made, it becomes important to identify the illness that caused the incurable wound mentioned by Jeremiah. In order to do this, it is necessary to look at the call of another prophet. When God called Isaiah to the prophetic ministry, he gave Isaiah a near impossible mission. God told Isaiah: "Go, and say to this people: 'Hear and hear, but do not understand; see and see, but do not perceive.' Make the heart of this people fat, and their ears heavy, and shut their eyes; lest they see with their eyes, and hear with their ears, and understand with their hearts, and turn and be healed" (Isa 6:9–10 RSV). God told Isaiah his preaching would harden

---

2. Keil, *The Prophecies of Jeremiah*, 1:182.

3. Rutledge, *Not Ashamed of the Gospel*, 352.

4. Fretheim, *Jeremiah*, 154.

5. Craigie, Kelley, and Drinkard, *Jeremiah 1–25*, 140.

the hearts of the people and they would not listen. The people's unbelief, their stubborn hearts, and their resistance to the prophet's words were caused by their rebellion against God.

According to the Lord's word to Isaiah, if the people would hear the message the prophet was to proclaim, if they would turn or repent, then they would be healed (v. 10). Thus, it is God who compares the rebellion of the people with spiritual illness. The rebellion of the people was worse than physical illness and only the message proclaimed by Isaiah could bring the people to repentance and to the healing of their wound. Thus, the balm of Gilead is a metaphor used by Jeremiah to explain how the people could find a cure for their spiritual illness. The balm that Jeremiah was talking about was not repentance, even though repentance was the first step toward the healing of their wound.

Several times in the Old Testament, the prophets speak about Judah's rebellion as an incurable wound. Hosea said: "When Ephraim saw his sickness, and Judah his wound, then Ephraim went to Assyria, and sent to the great king. But he is not able to cure you or heal your wound" (Hos 5:13). Isaiah said: "Why will you still be smitten, that you continue to rebel? The whole head is sick, and the whole heart faint. From the sole of the foot even to the head, there is no soundness in it, but bruises and sores and bleeding wounds; they are not pressed out, or bound up, or softened with oil" (Isa 1:5–6 RSV).

In the book of Jeremiah, the Lord spoke of Judah's illness and its incurable wound. Of Jerusalem, God said: "Her sickness and wounds are ever before me" (Jer 6:7). He also said: "For the wound of the daughter of my people is my heart wounded" (Jer 8:21 RSV).

Why was not the wound of God's people healed? Because the preaching of the false prophets did not provide the healing the people needed. God himself accused the prophets of not providing healing to the people. The Lord spoke these words about the prophets: "For from the least to the greatest of them, every one is greedy for unjust gain; and from prophet to priest, every one deals falsely. They have healed the wound of my people lightly, saying, 'Peace, peace,' when there is no peace" (Jer 6:13–14). The same words are repeated again in Jeremiah 8:10–11. God is saying the prophets have healed the wound of the people only lightly because they were preaching the wrong message.

"Is there no balm in Gilead? Is there no physician there? Why then is there no healing for the wound of my people?" (Jer 8:22). Jeremiah is proclaiming Judah is like a person who is sick or wounded. He is also proclaiming the balm of Gilead is the word of God in the mouth of the prophets and the prophets are the physicians sent by God to bring the medicine that could heal the spiritual wound of the people.

Thus, in Jeremiah 8:22, the prophet is saying there were plenty of physicians in Gilead who could heal the spiritual sickness of the people of Judah, for the physicians were the prophets. There was plenty of balm in Gilead, for the balm of Gilead in the mouth of Jeremiah is a metaphor for the word of God being preached by the prophets to a rebellious people. But there was no healing because the prophets were preaching a message that did not bring healing. The Lord is the great healer of Israel: "I am the LORD, your healer" (Exod 15:26). But healing would only come when the prophet faithfully proclaimed the word of God to the people.

The words of Jeremiah have a message for those who preach God's word. Those who speak on behalf of God proclaim their message through the power of the Holy Spirit that people's attitudes may be altered, lives may be changed, and transformation may occur. Those who preach are heralds of God's truth, proclaiming a message of hope to hungry souls and lonely hearts. Everyone who preaches must remember the words of the prophet Micah: "But I am full of the courage that the LORD's Spirit gives, and have a strong commitment to justice. This enables me to confront Jacob with its rebellion, and Israel with its sin" (Mic 3:8 NET).

41

The Mother of Seven

"THE MOTHER OF SEVEN will grow faint and breathe her last. She will die, ashamed and humiliated, while it is still daylight" (Jer 15:9). In ancient Israel, the symbolism of giving birth to seven children was used as a proverbial expression to describe a woman blessed with children or to refer to a family whose future in Israel was guaranteed because the family name would survive in the memory of the community through the sons. Two classic examples of "mother of seven" appear in the Old Testament. When Hannah was delivered from her barrenness and gave birth to Samuel, she said: "The barren has borne seven" (1 Sam 2:5). These words reflect Hannah's joy in becoming a mother and the awareness that she had conceived a son because of God's help. The second example is found in Ruth 4:15. After Ruth married Boaz and gave birth to Obed, the women of Bethlehem paid her the highest compliment by telling Naomi that her daughter-in-law Ruth was better "than seven sons." This recognition spoke highly of Ruth's character since being a mother of seven sons was the highest accolade a woman in Israel could receive.

For a woman, to be a mother and to have sons was to be blessed by God. Psalm 113:9 says the Lord should be praised because "He gives the barren woman a home, making her the joyous mother of children." On the other hand, women such as Sarah, Rebekah, Rachel, and Samson's mother were barren and unhappy. These women carried with them the sorrow of being unable to give children to their husbands and the opprobrium of their society for not being blessed by God.

In light of the positive sentiment the proverbial expression of being a mother of seven carried in Israel, it is significant that Jeremiah used the same imagery to describe the enormous tragedy and the depth of sorrow that would come to Jerusalem as a result of the judgment God was bringing upon the nation. During the invasion of Jerusalem, so many husbands would be killed that the widows of Jerusalem would become "more numerous than the sand of the seas." So many children would die that mothers would receive news that their sons were killed early in battle (Jer 15:8).

According to Jeremiah, when the judgment arrives upon Jerusalem and a mother of seven hears the news of the death of her children, that mother will be filled with anguish, tormented by the terrible deaths of her children. Robbed of her children in the prime of their lives, the woman grows faint, breathes her last, and dies (Hebrew: "breathes out her life"), ashamed and humiliated because she has lost her seven sons (Jer 15:9). The imagery of a mother of seven losing her children is used to describe the anguish, pain, and sorrow that will fall upon the inhabitants of Jerusalem. The imagery, although painful, is a good illustration of the paroxysms of emotion evoked by the disaster that came upon Judah in 587 B.C.

There is no greater human sorrow than the one that comes to a home when a mother of many children dies in the prime of her life, leaving her children deprived of maternal love. This is the imagery Jeremiah uses to describe the plight of the people of Judah. Jeremiah, anticipating the coming judgment that the Lord will bring upon Judah, uses the imagery of a husband mourning the death of his wife and the mother of his many children.

Mother Jerusalem (2 Sam 20:19) has lost her children and her judgment is a reversal of the promise God made to the ancestors. The promise of life God made to Abraham (Gen 22:17)—"I will indeed bless you, and I will make your offspring as numerous as the sand on the seashore"—now becomes the reality of death: "Their widows will be more numerous than the grains of sand on the seashore" (Jer 15:8).

The promise of life once made to Abraham has become an illustration of what will happen to Jerusalem when the destroyer comes. The city that once was full of people will now become like a widow deprived of her children (Lam 1:1). The proverbial expression used to describe a woman blessed with God's favor will now become the symbol of bereavement and death.

42

The Coming of the Messiah

INCORRECT INTERPRETATIONS OF DANIEL 9:25–27 have produced a type of theology exemplified by the teachings of the Scofield Bible, the rapture, the tribulation, and the Left Behind phenomenon. The problem with most books that adopt a premillennial interpretation of Daniel 9:25–27 is that they are based on the theology taught in the Scofield Bible.

When interpreting a text, the reader must take the interpretation that reflects the plain meaning of Scripture. It is possible to arrive at the original intent of the writer, even when the reader may not truly understand the author's message. When the biblical text is read and studied without any preconceived ideas, the plain meaning of the text can be discovered and the true message of the author can be understood. When this happens, then, in the end, readers honor the original intent of the writer of the biblical text. It is true that much of biblical scholarship today is not neutral. For instance, those who accept biblical criticism interpret the Pentateuch using the principles derived from source or tradition criticism. Those who uphold Mosaic authorship interpret the Pentateuch from the perspective that Moses wrote everything in the fifteenth century B.C.

The focus of this chapter is not solely on biblical interpretation, but on the translation of the text. From this perspective, it seems some English Bibles reflect a bias in the translation of some texts. I believe Daniel 9:25–27 is one of those texts. Before discussing Daniel 9:25–27, it is necessary to say a few words about translations and translators.

Translating the Hebrew text of the Old Testament into another language is a difficult task. Translating is difficult because the structure of one language is different from others and what makes sense in one language does not make sense in another. Another factor that makes translating difficult is that languages change from time to time. Language is always evolving to meet the challenges of culture, customs, religion, and politics. The English used by the translators of the King James Version in 1611 is different from the English used by people today.

Eugene Nida, in his book dealing with the science of translation, discusses the many challenges translators face. For instance, translators must use Hebrew dictionaries and grammar written in English. Thus, the structure of the English language is bound to be an influence in any translation, "regardless of the translator's wish to avoid 'linguistic contamination.'"[1] Nida notes that one basic requirement for translators is they must have empathy for the original author. The words translators must employ to translate a text are already set out for them by the original author. Using this empathetic spirit, translators must be like the original author; translators must not try to improve the original author. Nida writes that the translator "must exert every effort to reduce to a minimum any intrusion of himself which is not in harmony with the intent of the original author and message."[2] Nida also notes that at times, translators purposely and consciously "attempted to change a message in order to make it conform to his own . . . religious predilections." According to Nida, "These are particularly evident when a translator feels inclined to improve on the original, correct apparent errors, or defend a personal preference by slanting his choice of words."[3]

In light of Nida's views on translations and translators, I propose to study Daniel 9:25 using Nida's insights. In my discussion of Daniel 9:25, it does not matter whether one accepts that Daniel was written in the sixth century B.C. or in the second century B.C. An unbiased translation of this verse will produce the same result. The KJV reads: "Know therefore and understand, that from the going forth of the commandment to restore and to build Jerusalem unto the Messiah the Prince shall be seven weeks, and threescore and two weeks: the street shall be built again, and the wall, even in troublous times" (Dan 9:25). The translation "Messiah the Prince" is adopted by the ASV, the HCSB, the NASB, and others. The NIV has "the Anointed One, the ruler." Following the Septuagint, the DRA has "unto Christ the prince." It is clear the translators of this text slanted their choice of words in Daniel 9:25.

---

1. Nida, *Toward a Science of Translation*, 148.

2. Ibid., 154.

3. Ibid., 155.

The Hebrew word behind the word "Messiah" is *māshîaḥ*. The word means "anointed one" and is used to designate kings, priests, and even Cyrus, king of Persia (Isa 45:1).

The word translated "Prince" is *nāgîd*, a word that literally means "ruler" or "leader." The word is applied to people in the military, in government, and in religion. Thus, the word *nāgîd* refers to a captain in the army, to a king, and to a priest. Azariah, the high priest was called "the ruler [*nāgîd*] of the house of God" (2 Chr 31:13).

In Daniel 9:25 the word "the" as in "the Messiah," is not present in the Hebrew text. Thus, the Hebrew text is talking about "an anointed one," one who could be a priest or a king. However, because the translators of the KJV used the word "Messiah," with a definite article and a capital letter M, Christians immediately say: "there is only one person who is 'The Messiah,' and that person is Jesus Christ." Thus, readers of the KJV are predisposed by the translation to see Jesus Christ in Daniel 9:25. However, if one adopts the translation of the RSV, the whole idea of the text changes.

The RSV reads: "Know therefore and understand that from the going forth of the word to restore and build Jerusalem to the coming of an anointed one, a prince, there shall be seven weeks. Then for sixty-two weeks it shall be built again with squares and moat, but in a troubled time."

E. J. Young, in his commentary on Daniel, follows the translation of the RSV. He translates the words in question: "unto an anointed one, a prince." Now, this is a good translation. But then he inserts this comment: "The fact is that there is only One in history who fully satisfied the two essential requisites of the theocratic king, Jesus who is the Messiah."[4] Now, this is a bad (though some would say good) interpretation and this is the same principle that influenced translations of Daniel 9:25.

In discussing Daniel 9:25, I have not made any reference to date or authorship. This is irrelevant when it comes to the issue of translation. A commentator may inject his theological bias on the interpretation of the text and decide who that anointed one was. However, the translator does not have that luxury. The translator must follow the intent of the original author and avoid making the decision of who in history fully satisfies the two essentials of leadership mentioned in Daniel 9:25, as the translators of the King James did.

So, one may ask: who was the anointed one mentioned by Daniel? The answer to this question requires another study: it all depends on how the seventy weeks of Daniel is understood. Here again, I believe the

4. Young, *The Prophecy of Daniel*, 204.

translators of the King James allowed their view of Jesus to influence the translation of the text. In the next chapter I will present my understanding of the seventy weeks of Daniel.

I believe some interpreters bring their views and prejudices to the translation and interpretation of the biblical text. This is not the ideal situation because such a practice deprives many readers of the proper understanding of what the Bible says. This is the reason I believe the notes of the Scofield Bible are not helpful. Many good people, influenced by the notes of the Scofield Bible, have developed a system of theology that cannot stand the scrutiny of an impartial reading of the biblical text. I am convinced that if the Scofield notes had not been included, then the teachings of Scofield would have perished a long time ago.

43

The Seventy Weeks of Daniel

In this chapter I continue my study dealing with translation issues related to the controversial text of Daniel 9:25–27. The previous chapter, *The Coming of the Messiah*, dealt with the issue of how to translate the words "Messiah" (*māshîaḥ*) and "Prince" (*nāgîd*) in Daniel 9:25. The conclusion reached in the previous chapter was that the text requires the translation "an anointed one" and "a prince."

In the present chapter, I want to deal with another issue of translation: the seventy weeks of Daniel. The KJV translates Daniel 9:25–26 as follows: "Know therefore and understand, that from the going forth of the commandment to restore and to build Jerusalem unto the Messiah the Prince shall be seven weeks, and threescore and two weeks: the street shall be built again, and the wall, even in troublous times. After the sixty-two weeks, an anointed one shall be cut off and shall have nothing, and the troops of the prince who is to come shall destroy the city and the sanctuary." According to this translation, "the Messiah" shall come after sixty-nine weeks (seven weeks plus sixty-two weeks). However, Daniel 9:26 says that "the Messiah" shall be cut off at the end of sixty-two weeks. The same approach is taken by the HCSB. The HCSB reads: "Know and understand this: From the issuing of the decree to restore and rebuild Jerusalem until Messiah the Prince will be seven weeks and 62 weeks."

The problem with these two translations and others that follow the same reading is that they do not take into consideration the Hebrew accentuation of verse 25. The proper understanding of Hebrew accents is complicated, but a few words can clarify the issue. In Hebrew there are two types of accents and they act as punctuation marks. The strong accents serve as stops (periods), colons, and semicolons. One of these accents is called the *athnah*. The function of the *athnah* is to mark the first half of a verse and serves as a strong break within a sentence.

The Hebrew text of Daniel 9:25 contains an *athnah* under the Hebrew word for "seven," which in the text closes the first period of sevens. Thus, in the Hebrew text, the accent makes a separation between the two periods of weeks. If the translator of the KJV had followed the Hebrew accentuation, the translation of Daniel 9:25 would read as follows: "Know therefore and understand that from the going out of the word to restore and build Jerusalem to the coming of an anointed one, a prince, there shall be seven weeks. Then for sixty-two weeks it shall be built again with squares and moat, but in a troubled time." Then verse 26 adds: "And after the sixty-two weeks, an anointed one shall be cut off" (Dan 9:26 RSV).

This is the translation adopted by the ESV. The RSV and a few other translations have adopted similar reading. Notice that the coming of the anointed one occurs at the end of seven weeks, not at the end of sixty-nine weeks. The difference between the ESV and the KJV is that the ESV follows the Masoretic Text (MT) while the KJV follows the Greek translation of the Old Testament known as the Theodotion text.

The issue among interpreters is which text reflects the original reading of Daniel 9:25. Those who advocate the Theodotion reading do so because this translation was finished in the second century A.D., while the Masoretic text found its final form in the ninth or tenth century A.D. Many people believe the Masoretes changed the text to avoid the messianic interpretation of Daniel 9:25, whereas Theodotion's translation supports the messianic view.

Those who take the traditional translation of Daniel 9:25, represented by the King James Version and other translations, are led to believe that "the Messiah," "the Prince," was killed at the end of the sixty-ninth week. Since the words "Messiah," and the "Prince," are interpreted as Jesus, then the dates are calculated so that the conclusion of the sixty-ninth week ends in A.D. 32, the year Christ died.

This calculation leaves the last week, the seventieth week of Daniel, unfulfilled. This is where the dispensationalism of Scofield enters in. Since the seventieth week does not fit historically, dispensationalists talk about "The Great Parenthesis." As Ironside, a proponent of the theory, writes: "Between the sixty-nine and the seventieth weeks we have a Great Parenthesis which has now lasted over nineteen hundred years. The seventieth week has been postponed by God Himself, who changes the times and the seasons because of the transgression of the people."[1] According to this view, the reason the last week was postponed was because when Christ died on the cross, "the prophetic clock stopped" until the age of the church comes to an end.

This infusion of ideas *into* Daniel 9:25–27, a process that is called eisegesis, is what leads people into dispensationalism. Eisegesis is the process of interpreting the Bible in which the interpreter tries to make the Bible say something that is in accordance with some pre-existing idea about a particular issue or doctrine. Those who use eisegesis to interpret the Bible generally are not willing to allow the Bible to be understood as it was intended by the original writer. Rather, those who infuse ideas into the Bible are trying to prove something they already believe. People who use eisegesis can find aliens and astronauts in the Old Testament. They can also find America and Russia, Gorbachev and Saddam Hussein, the rapture and the tribulation, and a host of other things that are not in the Bible.

So, who was the anointed one of Daniel 9:25? In order to answer this question, there are several things that must control the interpretation of the text. Again, using the text of the ESV, the identification of the anointed one must fall within the guidelines outlined below.

First, an anointed one, who is also a prince of the community, must come at the end of the first seven weeks: "Know therefore and understand that from the going out of the word to restore and build Jerusalem to the coming of an anointed one, a prince, there shall be seven weeks" (v. 25a). Second, after the coming of the anointed one Jerusalem shall be built again: "Then for sixty-two weeks it shall be built again with squares and moat, but in a troubled time" (v. 25b). Third, at the end of the sixty-two weeks an anointed one shall be killed: "And after the sixty-two weeks, an anointed one shall be cut off and shall have nothing" (v. 26a). Fourth, after the death of the anointed one the people of a prince shall destroy the sanctuary: "And the people of the prince who is to come shall destroy the city and the sanctuary. Its end shall come with a flood, and to the end there shall be war. Desolations are decreed. And he shall make a strong covenant with many for one week, and for half of the week he shall put an end to sacrifice and offering. And on the wing of abominations shall come one who makes desolate, until the decreed end is poured out on the desolator" (vv. 26b–27).

When the biblical text is taken at face value, the text speaks of two anointed ones and two princes. Also, when the biblical text is taken at face value, the dispensationalism of Scofield, the Great Parenthesis, the

---

1. Ironside, *The Great Parenthesis*, 23.

seven-year tribulation, and all the other issues related to this doctrine, are found to have no biblical basis. As for the identity of the one who was a prince and an anointed one, I leave that for those who write commentaries. My intent was only to demonstrate how a biased translation of a text can lead people astray. Translators have a responsibility to be neutral in their translation of the biblical text.

44

The Knowledge of God

PREACHING IS NOT EASY. Preaching from the Old Testament is very difficult. The reason many pastors do not preach often from the Old Testament
is because they are not familiar with the society and culture of the people
who populate the pages of the Bible. Many pastors are also not familiar
with the original languages of the biblical text. The art of preaching requires
from the preacher a meticulous study of the biblical text.

Since many pastors do not know Hebrew, they depend on an English
translation to provide in their language what the original writers were trying to communicate in theirs. And here is where the problem begins. At
times, an idea in the biblical text cannot be easily transferred into English.
Thus, the reader may not understand all the nuances of a text as the original
writer intended. The worst-case scenario happens when translators of the
biblical text mistranslate the text or fail to convey the correct meaning of
the biblical text in their translations. In this case, the pastor who depends
on one English translation may fail to understand the real message the
original writer was trying to convey to his audience.

Many evangelical Christians use the NIV as their study Bible. In addition, many people whose first language is not English also use the NIV
because the language used in this translation is easy to understand. The
problem with the NIV is its inconsistency in translating words from Hebrew
to English. Most people in the pew will never notice the problems in the
NIV because they use only one translation. Most pastors will not notice the
problem either unless they read the biblical text in several different translations and compare them, or if they use an interlinear Hebrew-English Bible
to look at how Hebrew words are used in the translation of the text.

The following is one example taken from the book of Hosea. I will use the NIV first, and then compare the NIV translation with three other translations.

Hosea 4:1 (NIV): "Hear the word of the LORD, you Israelites, because the LORD has a charge to bring against you who live in the land: 'There is no faithfulness, no love, no acknowledgment of God in the land.'"

Here the NIV translates the Hebrew words *da'at 'ĕlōhîm* as "acknowledgment of God." The Hebrew word *da'at* means "knowledge." The expression *da'at'ĕlōhîm* is an expression used to describe the special relationship between God and Israel that comes out of the covenant binding Israel to God. When Hosea said Israel did not have knowledge of God, the prophet was declaring Israel had failed to abide by the demands of their covenantal relationship with God.

In English, the word used by the NIV, "acknowledgment," means "to admit the truth or fact of," and "a formal declaration of an act." The NIV translation seems to imply Israel was declaring there was no God in the land. The NIV translation is confusing because it does not clearly convey the intent of the original writer. Both the NRSV and the ESV have "knowledge of God." Only the NIV and TNIV have "acknowledgment."

In Hosea 4:6, the NIV reads: "My people are destroyed from lack of knowledge. Because you have rejected knowledge, I also reject you as my priests." Here the NIV translates the same word, *da'at*, as "knowledge." This translation is correct, because what the people lacked and what the people rejected was "knowledge," not "acknowledgment." The NRSV and the ESV translate the word *da'at* here as "knowledge" and so does the TNIV. However, both the NIV and the TNIV translated *da'at* as "acknowledgement" in Hosea 6:6.

This inconsistency of the NIV is troublesome because the average reader may not understand the usage of the same Hebrew words with different meanings in English. The average reader is certain to miss the emphasis the prophet was trying to convey by his use of *da'at*. Thus, people who read Hosea 4:1 in the NIV may fail to grasp the magnitude of the sins of Israel.

45

The Word *Ḥesed* in the Book of Hosea

In the previous chapter, I pointed out the inconsistency of the NIV in translating the word *da'at 'ĕlōhîm* in the book of the prophet Hosea. In that study I mentioned the problems interpreters have when using the NIV in trying to arrive at a proper understanding of the biblical text. In this chapter I want to review another inconsistency found in the NIV that, to me at least, obfuscates the original meaning of the biblical text and sends a confusing message to a reader who cannot read the biblical text in its original language.

Again, in my comparison, I will use three other translations. I will compare the NIV with the NRSV, the ESV, and the TNIV. I could have used other translations, but my focus is on the NIV. I use the NIV as the model for comparison since many evangelical Christians have chosen to use the NIV because of the simplified language it uses to convey the biblical message. To readers whose first language is not English, the NIV is easy to understand. However, because of the inconsistencies of the NIV, at times, the message it presents is not as clear as it should be.

Another example of inconsistency in the NIV's translation of the book of Hosea is found in the translation of the word *ḥesed*. The following is a translation of *ḥesed* in Hosea 4:1: "Hear the word of the LORD, you Israelites, because the LORD has a charge to bring against you who live in the land: 'There is no faithfulness, no love [*ḥesed*], no acknowledgment of God in the land'" (Hos 4:1 NIV).

In this verse, the NIV translates the word *ḥesed* as "love." The word *ḥesed* is difficult to translate into English because the word has a wealth of meanings in Hebrew. The correct understanding of *ḥesed* is attained only in a study of the context of where the word is used. However, as H. J. Zobel has shown in the *Theological Dictionary of the Old Testament*, "the one who receives an act of *ḥeseḏ* responds with a similar act of *ḥeseḏ*, or at least that the one who demonstrates *ḥeseḏ* is justified in expecting an equivalent act in return."[1]

In my study of the word *ḥeseḏ* in Isaiah, "All Their Goodliness," (chapter 36) I wrote: "The word *ḥeseḏ* is related to the covenant God established with Israel at Sinai. The word *ḥeseḏ* refers to the commitment that binds two parties to a relationship."

In his study of the word *ḥeseḏ* in the Hebrew Bible, Clark says *ḥeseḏ* is an "action performed, in the context of a deep and enduring commitment between two persons or parties."[2] Since faithfulness to a relationship is a character of God, God also expects his people to be as committed to the relationship as he is.

When the word is applied to God, it refers to his faithfulness to a relationship. Thus, the word is best translated as "faithfulness" or "unfailing love." When the word is applied to human beings, it refers to the loyalty and commitment people should bring to a relationship. In this case, a good translation of *ḥeseḏ* should be "commitment" "loyalty." A strong relationship is built on commitment. Israel should be as loyal and committed to the covenant as God was.

In Hosea 4:1, the NRSV translates *ḥeseḏ* as "loyalty," the ESV as "steadfast love," and the TNIV as "love." Love or steadfast love is a good translation, but "loyalty" is a better translation. On the other hand, the NIV translates the same word, *ḥeseḏ*, as "mercy" in Hosea 6:6: "For I desire mercy, not sacrifice, and acknowledgment of God rather than burnt offerings" (Hos 6:6 NIV). In this verse the translations differ: The NRSV has "For I desire steadfast love." The ESV translates "For I desire steadfast love" and the TNIV translates "For I desire mercy." In my opinion, the HCSB has a better translation: "For I desire loyalty."

The word "mercy" in the NIV does not convey in English what the biblical author was trying to communicate to his audience. In English, the word "mercy" means a compassionate treatment of a person, to be kind or forgiving to someone. This is not what the biblical writer was trying to convey to his readers. If the NIV had been consistent and used "love" here as it used it in 4:1, the translation would be acceptable and the message would convey the intent of the writer. However, the inconsistency of the NIV leaves the reader at a loss because he or she will believe what the Lord

---

1. Zobel, "*ḥeseḏ*," in *TDOT* 5:47.
2. Clark, *The Word Hesed*, 267.

requires from his people is that they be compassionate to fellow Israelites, when in reality God was requiring the people's loyalty to the relationship established by the covenant.

In Hosea 12:6 the NIV translates *hesed* as "love" and in Hosea 10:12 the NIV translates *hesed* as "unfailing love." At least "unfailing love" in the NIV is better than "kindness" in the ASV, "piety" in the NAB, and "goodness" in the TNK.

There are several lessons to be learned here by pastors and seminary students who do not know Hebrew. The first lesson is pastors and seminary students must consult more than one translation when studying the biblical text. Check several translations and compare how the biblical text is translated. Second, they also must consult good exegetical commentaries. Since translations differ, commentaries will also differ. A good exegetical commentary will provide a brief study of the meaning of important theological words in the text. The third and final lesson is that it is never too late to study biblical languages. No one needs to be a scholar in Hebrew or Greek, but a basic knowledge of the language will help pastors and students know how to consult an interlinear translation of the biblical text or check the meaning of specific words in a Hebrew or Greek lexicon. When it comes to biblical translations, the saying remains true: "trust, but verify."

46

The Word "Justice" in Amos

THE MESSAGE OF AMOS contains a strong criticism of the royal officials of the Northern Kingdom and those who administered justice in the courts because they were undermining the legal system of Israel in order to exploit the underprivileged and drive the peasants away from their patrimony. Because of the legal decisions made by dishonest judges, many landowners became tenants of a rich class of people who abused the legal system to take possession of their lands.

Amos used the word "justice" (*mishpāṭ*) to criticize the royal officials, the judges, and the rich for the perversion of the judicial process in Israel. In his commentary on Amos, James L. Mays writes: "In Amos *mishpāṭ* is specifically associated with the court in the gates and means the judicial process and its decisions by which right order is maintained in social relations, and especially the protection of [the] weak and poor through the help of the court."[1] Mays also said: "When the poor and afflicted come to the courts of justice they are dealt out the very same injustice from which they sought relief. To Amos, who will allow Israel no other identity and way of life than that given her in the election of Yahweh, such a reversal of things staggers the mind, and he can only compare it to some incredible perversion of the normal order of things."[2]

The word "justice" (*mishpāṭ*) appears four times in the book of Amos: three times the word appears in association with "righteousness" (*ṣedāqâ*) and once the word appears alone:

1. Mays, *Amos*, 108.
2. Ibid., 121.

"O you who turn justice (*mishpāṭ*) to wormwood, and cast down righteousness (*ṣedāqâ*) to the earth (Amos 5:7 RSV).

"But let justice (*mishpāṭ*) roll down like waters, and righteousness (*ṣedāqâ*) like an ever-flowing stream (Amos 5:24 RSV).

"But you have turned justice (*mishpāṭ*) into poison and the fruit of righteousness (*ṣedāqâ*) into wormwood" (Amos 6:12 RSV).

"Hate evil, and love good, and establish justice (*mishpāṭ*) in the gate" (Amos 5:15 RSV).

Anyone who desires to understand the message of Amos should read the book in light of Amos's emphasis on social justice. A study of the word "justice" as it appears in the book of Amos will help the reader see Amos as a prophet who spoke against evil in the public place. Unfortunately, the NIV is not a good place to go for a study of the word "justice" in Amos. The reason for this statement is that the NIV is not consistent in its use of the word "justice" in the book of Amos. Twice the NIV uses the word "justice" in places where the word *mishpāṭ* does not appear in the Hebrew text. Those readers of the Bible who do not know Hebrew will think the word "justice" in those additional places has the same meaning as the word "justice" in the verses where the Hebrew word *mishpāṭ* appears.

In Amos 2:7, the NIV reads: "They trample on the heads of the poor as upon the dust of the ground and deny justice to the oppressed." The Hebrew should be translated as follows: "They turn aside the way of the afflicted." This translation is followed by the RSV: "they that trample the head of the poor into the dust of the earth, and turn aside the way of the afflicted."

The NIV uses the word "justice" and translates the expression "to turn aside the way" by "deny justice" even though Amos did not use the word *mishpāṭ*. Wolff says the Hebrew expression "to turn aside the way of the afflicted" "is an abbreviated equivalent of 'to pervert the courses of justice.'"[3] Mays writes that to "'turn aside the way of the afflicted' is a locution for the perversion of legal procedure. 'Way' (*derek*) is a synonym for 'justice' (*mishpāṭ*)."[4]

Only the NIV and the TNIV use the word "justice" in Amos 2:7. All other translations do not use the word "justice" to clarify the message of Amos. In Amos 5:12, the NIV reads: "There are those who oppress the innocent and take bribes and deprive the poor of justice in the courts." The Hebrew should

3. Wolff, *Joel and Amos*, 166.
4. Mays, *Amos*, 46.

be translated as follows: "You who oppress the righteous, who take a bribe, and turn aside the needy in the gate." This translation is followed by the RSV: "you who afflict the righteous, who take a bribe, and turn aside the needy in the gate." The NIV, by using the word "justice" here, is following a common practice in the Hebrew Bible where the verb *nāṭah* ("to turn aside") usually occurs together with the word *mishpāṭ* (Exod 23:6; Deut 16:19; Prov 17:23). However, although the word *nāṭah* is used, the word *mishpāṭ* does not appear in Amos 5:12. Only the NIV, the TNIV, the NET, the HCSB, and the NLT use the word "justice" in Amos 5:12. The NKJV also uses "justice," but the word is in italics to indicate that it is not in the Hebrew text and has been added to clarify the meaning of the English translation.

What distinguishes Amos and his use of *mishpāṭ* is that he is the first prophet to use the word together with *ṣedāqâ*. As Wolff has pointed out, "this word pair is completely unknown in Israel's legal collections in the Pentateuch."[5] After Amos, Isaiah used the words *mishpāṭ* and *ṣedāqâ* together three times (Isa 1:21; 5:7; 28:17). The two words again appear in wisdom literature, in the Psalms, and in Jeremiah. Wolff concludes that the use of the words *mishpāṭ* and *ṣedāqâ* in the Hebrew Bible clearly indicates that Amos was the first person to use them together.

By using the word "justice" in Amos 2:7 and 5:12, the NIV is trying to clarify to its readers the legal meaning behind these two verses. However, in doing so, the NIV may leave the impression in the mind of some readers that the Hebrew word *mishpāṭ* is behind the translation of "justice" in Amos 2:7 and 5:12.

Any translation of the Bible must clarify the original text for its readers, but, at times, the inconsistency of the NIV does not help the English-speaking reader grasp the significance of the use or non-use of specific words by the prophet. Some may see in the NIV an example of moderation and others may call the TNIV "maligned"; I would call both translations inconsistent.

5. Wolff, *Joel and Amos*, 245.

47

"What the Lord Requires"

MICAH 6:8 IS A verse very familiar to students of the Bible because it describes what God requires of his followers. The context of this verse, Micah 6:1–8, contains words connected with the court of law in ancient Israel. In the Old Testament, it was common for the elders of a city to come together and hold court in open places near the city gate (Amos 5:10; Ruth 4:1). At these gatherings, the people came to the elders for legal decisions. In these local courts, legal procedures and language were used and the proceedings would be familiar to most people. When addressing the people of Judah, Micah used the language of the courts, and his listeners understood the seriousness of the charges brought against them.

When Micah spoke to the people, he used the word *rib*. The verbal form of the word *rib* is used in Micah 6:1 and it is translated *plead your case*. The noun form of the word occurs twice in Micah 6:2 and it is translated *lawsuit* and (legal) *case*. With these words Micah is acting as Yahweh's lawyer in a covenantal lawsuit, indicating that Yahweh had a legal case against his people.

The Lawyer Summons the People to Court

"Now listen to what the LORD is saying: Rise, plead your case before the mountains, and let the hills hear your voice. Listen to the LORD's lawsuit, you mountains and enduring foundations of the earth, because the LORD has a case against His people, and He will argue it against Israel" (Mic 6:1–2 HCSB). Micah begins the Lord's case against Israel by calling the mountains to be witnesses in the legal proceedings. In the covenants known in the ancient Near East, the gods were called as witnesses to verify a violation of the covenant. Since Israel was not allowed to have other gods before Yahweh, the everlasting foundations of the earth served as witnesses of God's case against Israel.

Yahweh Presents His Case

"O my people, what have I done to you? In what have I wearied you? Answer me! For I brought you up from the land of Egypt, and redeemed you from the house of slavery; and I sent before you Moses, Aaron, and Miriam. O my people, remember now what King Balak of Moab devised, what Balaam son of Beor answered him, and what happened from Shittim to Gilgal, that you may know the saving acts of the LORD" (Mic 6:3–5). Yahweh presents his case by reminding the people of how much he did for them. He delivered them from the oppressive life they lived in Egypt; he delivered them from the house of slavery; he sent them three great leaders to help them on their journey from Egypt to Canaan; and he delivered them from the hands of Balak, king of Moab, and from the curses of Balaam, the false prophet. Yahweh did all these things so the people might appreciate his mighty work. After Yahweh presented his case, the people presented their defense.

The People Present Their Defense

"With what shall I come before the LORD, and bow myself before God on high? Shall I come before him with burnt offerings, with calves a year old? Will the LORD be pleased with thousands of rams, with ten thousands of rivers of oil? Shall I give my firstborn for my transgression, the fruit of my body for the sin of my soul?" (Mic 6:6–7). In their minds the people believed they had already done enough. They had brought sacrifices to the temple and made their offerings to God. Now they asked the prophet what else they needed to do. "What else must I do to show proper respect to God?" The people wondered what else God was requiring of them: more offerings and more yearling calves? Do we need to give to God thousands of rams? Or olive oil in abundance? Or even the sacrifice of our firstborn child?

The Lawyer Presents the Verdict

"He has showed you, O man, what is good. And what does the LORD require of you? To act justly and to love mercy and to walk humbly with your God" (Mic 6:8 NIV 1984). After both cases were presented, the prophet presented the decision of the court. What the Lord wanted was not more sacrifices or elaborate rituals. Rather, Micah declared what the Lord required of his people: "He has showed you, O man, what is good. And what does the LORD require of you? To act justly and to love mercy and to walk humbly with your God."

The issue raised by Micah was that Israel had rejected the good. This was the same accusation brought by Hosea against the people of the Northern Kingdom: "Israel has rejected what is good" (Hos 8:3). What Hosea and Micah were declaring to the people was that they had abandoned the requirements Yahweh had imposed on the nation. These requirements involved the people's social and moral responsibilities toward each other and toward God.

Micah rejected the suggestions made by the people that more sacrifices and offerings would please Yahweh. He also rebuked the people for their failure to understand what God demanded from his followers. Micah's words are similar to Hosea's exhortation to Israel: "So now, come back to your God! Act on the principles of love and justice, and always live in confident dependence on your God" (Hos 12:6 NLT).

The first requirement, "to act justly," refers to the moral obligation that existed among the members of the covenant community. The expression "O man" has been understood to have a universal application, that is, it applies to people everywhere. But the prophet was not addressing humanity in general; he was exhorting people who followed God. Justice was expected of those people who were joined together in a community bound by the bonds of the covenant. To do justice is to do what is right according to the demands stipulated in the covenant between God and Israel.

The third requirement, "To walk humbly with God," refers to a way of life in which an individual does not live independently of God but lives within the will and ways of God. This expression also means to live in a personal relationship with God. Enoch walked with God (Gen 5:22) and so did Noah (Gen 6:9).

It is the second requirement that demands an explanation. The Lord requires his followers "to love mercy." But, what does it mean "to love mercy"? The English dictionary defines "mercy" as "the compassionate or kindly forbearance shown toward an offender," "pity," "benevolence," and "an act of kindness or compassion." However, here Micah is not saying the Lord is requiring "kindness" or "pity." The Lord requires these things from his followers, but not in Micah 6:8.

The word "mercy" is a translation of the Hebrew *ḥesed*. The word *ḥesed* is used in the Old Testament to describe God's faithful commitment to Israel even when the nation was unfaithful to God. The word is also used to describe the conduct God expected from each Israelite: "For I desire loyalty and not sacrifice" (Hos 6:6 HSCB). In most contexts where the word *ḥesed* appears in the Old Testament, the word carries the idea of "commitment," "faithfulness," "loyalty."

So, what God requires of his followers is not sacrifice or something material that can be quantified and understood as a way of bribing God. What God requires of his people is faithfulness and commitment to the relationship established by the covenant. He requires the giving of one's life to him and to his way of life and that one should rejoice in living that kind of life. What God requires is not doing good for good's sake. What God requires of his followers is that they be committed and love being committed to God.

If the word *ḥesed* in Micah 6:8 is translated as "commitment" or "loyalty," then Micah 6:8 would read as follow: "He has showed you, O man, what is good. And what does the LORD require of you? To act justly and to love commitment [or "love being committed"] and to walk humbly with your God." Loving commitment to God is what God requires of his followers.

Bibliography

Allen, David L. *Hebrews*. New American Commentary. Nashville: B. & H. Academic, 2010.

Andersen, Francis I., and David N. Freedman. *Micah*. Anchor Bible. New York: Doubleday, 2000.

Barnes, Albert. *Isaiah*. Notes on the Old Testament. Grand Rapids: Baker, 1968.

Boling, Robert. *Judges*. Anchor Bible. Garden City: Doubleday, 1975.

Botterweck G. Johannes. "*keleḇ*." In *TDOT* 7:146–57.

Botterweck, G. Johannes, and Helmer Ringgren, editors. *Theological Dictionary of the Old Testament*. 15 vols. Grand Rapids: Eerdmans, 1995–2006.

Bright, John. *A History of Israel*. 4th edition. Philadelphia: Westminster, 2000.

Brown, Francis, S. R. Driver, and Charles A. Briggs. *A Hebrew and English Lexicon of the Old Testament*. Oxford: Clarendon, 1907.

Brueggemann, Walter. *Genesis*. Interpretation. Atlanta: John Knox, 1982.

Bullock, C. Hassell. *An Introduction to the Old Testament Poetical Books*. Chicago: Moody, 1988.

Bunyan, John. *Pilgrim's Progress*. Boston: D. Lothrop Company, 1893.

Carlson, Richard F., and Tremper Longman III. *Science, Creation and the Bible: Reconciling Rival Theories of Origin*. Downers Grove, IL: IVP Academic, 2010.

Cassuto, U. *A Commentary on the Book of Genesis*. Jerusalem: Magnes, 1961.

Cheyne, T. K. *The Prophecies of Isaiah*. New York: Thomas Whittaker, 1884.

Clarke, Adam. "Judges." *The Holy Bible: Commentary and Critical Notes*. Baltimore: John J. Harrod, 1834.

Clark, Gordon. *The Word Hesed in the Hebrew Bible*. Sheffield: Sheffield Academic, 1993.

Cogan, Mordechai, and Hayim Tadmor. *II Kings*. Anchor Yale Bible Commentaries. New Haven, CT: Yale University Press, 1988.

Craigie, Peter C. *Psalms 1–50*. Revised edition. Word Bible Commentary. Waco: Word, 2004.

Craigie, Peter C., Page H. Kelley, and Joel F. Drinkard Jr. *Jeremiah 1–25*. Word Bible Commentary. Dallas: Word, 1991.

Dahood, Michael. *Psalms 1–50*. Anchor Bible. New York: Doubleday, 1965.

DeHann, M. R. *Portraits of Christ in Genesis*. Grand Rapids: Zondervan, 1966.

Delitzsch, Franz. *Biblical Commentary on the Psalms*. Edinburgh: T. & T. Clark, 1871.

———. *A New Commentary on Genesis*. Minneapolis: Klock & Klock, 1888.

Ewald, H. *Commentary on the Psalms*. Edinburgh: Williams and Norgate, 1880.

Fretheim, Terence. *Jeremiah*. Smyth & Helwys Bible Commentary. Macon, GA: Smyth & Helwys, 2002.

Fuller, Thomas. *Selections from the Writings of Thomas Fuller*. London: The Religious Tract Society, 1865.

Gesenius, Wilhelm. *Gesenius' Hebrew Grammar*. Edited by E. Kautzsch. Translated by A. E. Cowley. 2nd edition. Oxford, 1910.

Goldingay, John. *Old Testament Theology: Israel's Gospel*. Vol. 1. Downers Grove, IL: InterVarsity, 2003.

Goslinga, C. J. *Joshua, Judges, Ruth*. Bible Student's Commentary. Grand Rapids: Zondervan, 1986.

Gottwald, Norman K. *The Hebrew Bible: A Socio-Literary Introduction*. Philadelphia: Fortress, 1985.

Gray, John. *I & II Kings*. Old Testament Library. Philadelphia: Westminster, 1970.

Hamilton, Victor P. *Handbook on the Pentateuch: Genesis, Exodus, Leviticus, Numbers, Deuteronomy*. Grand Rapids: Baker, 1982.

———. *The Book of Genesis: Chapters 1–17*. New International Commentary on the Old Testament. Grand Rapids: Eerdmans, 1990.

Henry, Matthew. "Judges." In *Matthew Henry's Commentary on the Whole Bible*. New York: Revell, n.d.

Hertzberg, Hans W. *I & II Samuel*. Old Testament Library. Philadelphia: Westminster, 1976.

Horton, T. C., and Charles E. Hurlburt. *The Wonderful Names of Our Wonderful Lord*. Uhrichsville, OH: Barbour and Company, 1996.

Ironside, H. A. *The Great Parenthesis: The Mystery in Daniel's Prophecy*. Grand Rapids: Zondervan, 1943.

Josephus, Flavius. *Josephus: Complete Works*. Translated by William Whiston. Reprint. Grand Rapids: Kregel, 1969.

Kaiser, Otto. *Isaiah 1–12: A Commentary*. Old Testament Library. Philadelphia: Westminster, 1983.

Keil, C. F. *Joshua, Judges, Ruth*. Biblical Commentary on the Old Testament. Grand Rapids: Eerdmans, 1950.

———. *The Books of Samuel*. Biblical Commentary on the Old Testament. Grand Rapids: Eerdmans, 1950.

———. *The Prophecies of Jeremiah*. Biblical Commentary on the Old Testament. 2 vols. Grand Rapids: Eerdmans, 1950.

Klein, Ralph. *1 Samuel*. Word Bible Commentary. Waco: Word, 1983.

Klein, William W., Craig L. Blomberg, and Robert L. Hubbard, Jr. *Introduction to Biblical Interpretation*. Dallas: Word, 1993.

Koehler, Ludwig, and Walter Baumgartner. *Lexicon in Veteris Testamenti Libros*. Leiden: E. J. Brill, 1958.

Kraus, Hans-Joachim. *Psalms 1–59*. Continental Commentary. Minneapolis: Fortress, 1993.

Leupold, H. C. *Exposition of Genesis*. Grand Rapids: Baker, 1965.

Mays, James L. *Amos*. Old Testament Library. Philadelphia: Westminster, 1969.

McCarter, P. Kyle Jr. *I Samuel*. Anchor Bible. New York: Doubleday, 1980.

———. *II Samuel*. Anchor Bible. New York: Doubleday, 1984.

Miller, Patrick D. *Interpreting the Psalms*. Philadelphia: Fortress, 1986.

Milton, John. *The Prose Works of John Milton*. London: Westley and Davis, 1834.

Mitchell, H. G. *Isaiah: A Study of Chapters I–XII*. New York: Crowell, 1897.

Moulton, Richard G. *The Modern Reader's Bible*. New York: Macmillan, 1935.

Nida, Eugene. *Toward a Science of Translation*. Leiden: E. J. Brill, 1964.

Ohler, Annemarie. *Studying the Old Testament: From Tradition to Canon*. Edinburgh: T. & T. Clark, 1985.

Pink, Arthur W. *Gleanings in Genesis*. Chicago: Moody, 1964.

Rad, Gerhard von. *Genesis: A Commentary*. Old Testament Library. Philadelphia: Westminster, 1961.

Ramm, Bernard. *Protestant Biblical Interpretation*. Grand Rapids: Baker, 1970.

Random House Dictionary of the English Language, The. New York: Random House, 1966.

Rutledge, Fleming. *Not Ashamed of the Gospel*. Grand Rapids: Eerdmans, 2007.

Sailhamer, John. "Genesis." *The Expositor's Bible Commentary*. Grand Rapids: Zondervan, 1990.

Schmidt, H. *Die Psalmen*. Tübingen: Mohr, 1934.

Skinner, John. *Genesis*. International Critical Commentary. New York: Scribner, 1910.

Smith, Duane E. "Pisser against a Wall: An Echo of Divination in Biblical Hebrew." *Catholic Biblical Quarterly* 72 (2010) 699–717.

Sumney, Jerry L. *The Bible: An Introduction*. Minneapolis: Fortress, 2010.

Trible, Phyllis. *Texts of Terror*. Overtures to Biblical Theology. Fortress, 1984.

Tullock, John. *The Old Testament Story*. 2nd edition. Englewood Cliff, NJ: Prentice-Hall, 1981.

Wenham, Gordon J. *Genesis 1–15*. Word Bible Commentary. Waco: Word, 1987.

Westermann, Claus. *Isaiah 40–66*. Old Testament Library. Philadelphia: Westminster, 1960.

———. *Genesis 1–11*. Continental Commentary. Minneapolis: Fortress, 1984.

Wolff, Hans W. *Joel and Amos*. Hermeneia. Philadelphia: Fortress, 1969.

Young, E. J. *The Prophecy of Daniel*. Grand Rapids: Eerdmans, 1949.

Zobel, H. J. "*ḥesed*." In *TDOT* 5:44–64.

Subjects

Subjects

Authors

Scriptures and Other Ancient Documents

Hebrew Bible/Old Testament

Genesis

1	3–6	13:17	23–24
1:1—2:4a	4	14	20
1:11	13	14:14–17	20
1:24–25	4	14:14	20–22
1:26–28	87	14:18	59, 69
1:26–27	88	15:7	23
2	3–6	15:20	18
2:4	4	16:10	13
2:7	4	17:8	23
2:16–17	7	19:12	104
2:17	7–9	22	27, 56
2:18	5	22:7	27
2:19	3–6	22:8	27
2:20	5	22:17	143
3:1	15	23	24
3:3	7	25:3	39
3:4–5	7	25:21	59
3:6	7	26:3	24
3:15	11–16	28:13	24
3:22	7–8	29:29	29
5:4	104	29:30	59
5:5	7	30:1	104
5:22	162	30:3–8	29
6:1–4	18	30:6	20
6:4	17–19	31:28	104
6:9	162	31:47	xvii
11:30	59	32:4—36:43	30
12:1	23	35:19	29
12:6	23	35:21	29
12:7	13, 26	35:22	29–31
13:15	23	36:6	104
		37:25	139
		38:24	44

3:10	60
3:15–16	58
3:15	58
3:16	58
4:1	160
4:12	60
4:13	59–61
4:15	142
4:17	59

1 Samuel

1:2	59
1:11–28	56
1:11	104
2:5	142
2:20	13
3:1	106–7
3:20	21
4:1–11	79
7:2	65
13:1	64–66
13:2	65
13:8–14	62
15:1–11	62
15:17	63
18:6	49
25	74
25:3	75
25:10	74
25:22	72, 74
25:34	72

2 Samuel

3:2–5	95
5:5	65
5:6–10	68
5:9	68
5:13	95
6:1–15	65
7	11, 95
7:14–16	79
7:16	12
8:17	94
8:18	69–70
16:9	76
18:18	105
20:1	79

20:19	143
21:19	56
21:22	18
24:6	21–22

1 Kings

1:3–4	109
4:5	71
5:1	94
10:18	95
11:1	94
11:4–7	78
11:7	53
11:9	78
11:14	78
11:23	78
11:26	78
11:28	79, 81
11:29	80
11:31	80
11:40	80
14:10–11	75
14:10	72
15:20	22
16:4	75
16:11	75
16:31	68, 95
21:21	75
21:24	75
22:39	95

2 Kings

8:18	95, n. 2
8:26	95, n.2
9:8	75
9:10	75
9:36	75
15:29	116
16:7	116
16:8	116
16:9	116

1 Chronicles

26:4–5	103

40:3–4	124
40:3	122–24
40:6	126–28
40:9	129–30
45:1	146
49:14	136
49:19	136
50:1	132, 134
54:7	136
62:4	136–37
62:5	136

Jeremiah

2:7	117
3:1	44
3:8	134
6:7	140
6:13–14	140
8:10–11	140
8:21	140
8:22	138, 140–141
10:11	xvii
15:8	143
15:9	142–43
15:21	121
34:22	136
46:11	139

Lamentations

| 1:1 | 143 |
| 2:9 | 107 |

Ezekiel

3:17	103
7:26	107
18:20	84
29:3	100
36:35	136

Daniel

2:4—7:28	xvii
9:25–27	144, 148, 150
9:25–26	148
9:25	145–46, 148–50
9:26	148–49
11:30	39

Hosea

4:1	153, 154–55
4:3	117
4:6	107, 153
5:13	140
6:4	128
6:6	153, 155, 163
8:3	162
10:12	156
12:6	156, 162

Amos

2:7	158–59
3:15	95
5:7	158
5:10	160
5:12	158–59
5:15	158
5:24	158
6:12	158
8:12	107

Micah

3:8	141
6:1–8	160
6:1–2	160
6:1	160
6:2	160
6:3–5	161
6:4	32–34
6:6–7	161
6:7	53
6:8	160, 162–63

Nahum

| 1:1 | 106 |

Zephaniah

| 1:13 | 103 |

Malachi

| 2:16 | 134 |

New Testament

Apocryphal Books

Printed in Great Britain
by Amazon